New York Giants
PRIDE

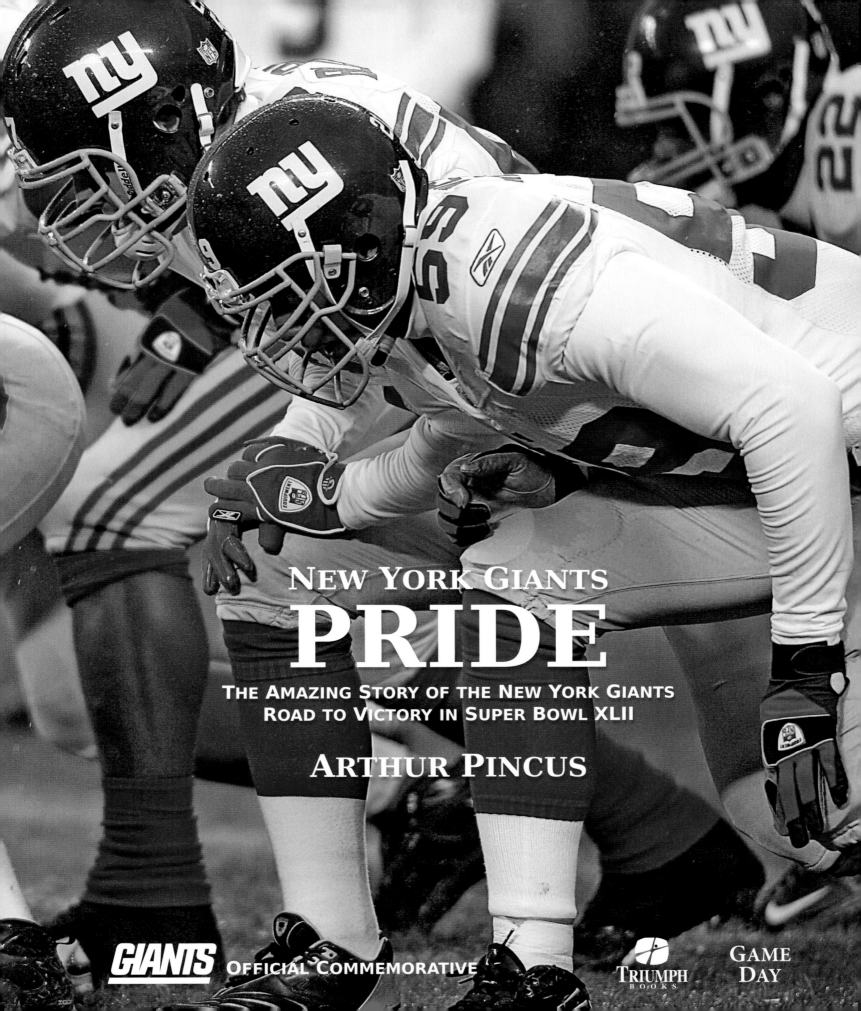

NEW YORK GIANTS
PRIDE

THE AMAZING STORY OF THE NEW YORK GIANTS ROAD TO VICTORY IN SUPER BOWL XLII

ARTHUR PINCUS

GIANTS OFFICIAL COMMEMORATIVE

TRIUMPH
BOOKS

GAME
DAY

Copyright © 2008 by GameDay Publishing.

Contributors

For the New York Giants: Michael Eisen

Managing editor: David McConnachie

Photo editor: Eric Zweig

Design and Production: Dan Diamond

Research: Chip Schrager

Copy editor: Charles Wilkins

Additional design: Larry Reid, Off the Map Studio

Printing: Kromar Printing., Winnipeg, Manitoba, Canada

Project Management: Dan Diamond and Associates, Inc., Toronto, Ontario

Photo Credits: see page 159

Distribution

This book is available in quantity at special discounts for your group or organization, for further information, contact:

Corporate and Special Sales:

Game Day Publishing, 11 Allstate Parkway, Markham, Ontario L3R 9T8   905/947-0491; Fax 905/947-4303;
dmcconnachie@gamedaylmc.com

Book Trade sales and distribution:

Triumph Books, 542 South Dearborn Street, Chicago, Illinois 60605   312/939-3330; Fax 312/663-3557

ISBN 978-1-60078-216-9

"The main ingredient of stardom is the rest of the team."
— Coach John Wooden, UCLA

To Giant fans everywhere and to my giant fans
Ellen, Alisa, Suzanne, Violet, David and Dan.

This book honors the legacy and memory of
Wellington Mara and Preston Robert Tisch.
If fans get the team owners they deserve,
we Giants' fans have been the luckiest of all.

Acknowledgments

Major appreciation must go to Chip Schrager, who gathered so much information so well in so short a time. To Allan Turowetz, David McConnachie and Dan Diamond, partners in this project. To Charles Wilkins, a thoughtful and sensitive editor. To Chris Pope, fan, friend and ace photographer. To Mary Safar who made the first suggestion. To great Giants fans—Eric Kennedy, Jay Rosenstein and Marc Zwerdling and all the members of BigBlueInteractive.com. To nfl.com and pro-football-reference.com for fine-grain statistics.

Tom Callahan's book *"The GM"* was the perfect starting point for this book as were the conversations we had.

A particular note of thanks to the Giants' communications staff, so professionally led by Pat Hanlon and Peter John-Baptiste. Many thanks as well to Michael Eisen and the staff of the Giants' excellent website www.giants.com.

And to the players and coaches and management of the 2007 New York Giants.

GIANTS

Dear Giants Fans,

The 2007 season for the New York Giants delivered many wonderful surprises and culminated with the team's victory over the previously-unbeaten Patriots in Super Bowl XLII.

This book—*New York Giants PRIDE*—takes us inside the huddle and onto the field as the team grew from contender to champion. The entire journey is described and depicted, from off-season moves that helped prepare for a future that came earlier than expected, to the joy shared by players and fans during a victory parade through the Canyon of Heroes.

And, at its very core, this book explains the power of *Giants PRIDE*, that consistent culture of excellence that has been central to Giants football since 1925. George Martin, who played 14 seasons with the Giants, describes it as the club's commitment to building an organization made up of people who possess both great athletic ability and strength of character.

The 2007 New York Giants embodied our club's guiding principle and provided a storybook ending to an incredible season. The organization is delighted to have been able to share this with the best sports fans in the world.

It is our hope that *New York Giants PRIDE* adds another page to the history and legacy of our beloved team.

Sincerely,

John Mara

Steve Tisch

NEW YORK GIANTS
PRIDE

TABLE OF CONTENTS

Coach Tom Coughlin's commitment to Giants Pride has been at the core of how the team has been run and built.

IN SEARCH OF NEW YORK GIANTS PRIDE

To COACH TOM COUGHLIN THE WORDS "NEW YORK GIANTS PRIDE" are tied to the entire history of the National Football League.

When he was named to his job in January 2004, those words were among his first: "What we must be all about now is the restoration of pride, of self pride, of team pride, the restoration of our professionalism and the dignity with which we conduct our business. We must replace despair with hope and return the energy and passion to New York Giants football."

Very soon the players got his message.

"When I signed with the Giants in March 2004," Shaun O'Hara recalled, "the first meeting we had as a team, that's what Coach talked about—New York Giants Pride. He was adamant. He had a whole new team with all new coaches, and he made sure we knew it.

"He said, 'I don't know how many games we're going to win but this is the greatest franchise in the history of the NFL.' He wanted everyone to understand that it's not just another team."

That first team under Tom Coughlin did not win that often, but one moment at the end of that season stuck with O'Hara. It came in the final two minutes of the season finale against Dallas. Both teams were out of the playoffs. The Giants trailed when they got the ball at their 34. The rookie quarterback Eli Manning led them downfield as if the Super Bowl championship depended on it. The result was a three-yard touchdown run by Tiki Barber and a 28-24 Giants victory, Eli's first as a Giant.

"That game, that drive, that play," O'Hara recalled. "That's all we were playing for was pride."

Coach Tom Coughlin didn't invent New York Giants Pride; he restored it. Harry Carson, the Giants captain during their Super Bowl season of 1986, said: "When I played it was a privilege to play for the

New York Giants, to be around guys like Rosey Brown, Emlen Tunnell, Andy Robustelli, Frank Gifford and Y.A. Tittle, who were synonymous with the Giants. I tried to pick up where those guys left off."

And one more thing, Carson said: "There's always been a certain sense of Giants Pride with the Giants defense."

So if you take pride in defense, combine it with the pride of past triumphs, add in players who are playing for one another and the image starts to take shape.

George Martin, another defensive star of the Super Bowl XXI champions, said New York Giants Pride came from the longtime owner and team president Wellington Mara. "Mr. Mara wanted great athletes on the field of play," Martin said, "but even more he wanted great people on the field of life."

Lawrence Tynes, a Giant of newer vintage, said he started to understand the feeling of New York Giants Pride soon after joining the team in a May 2007 trade. "It's a tough, hard-nosed team," the placekicker said, "but it's human. I always feel with John Mara and Steve Tisch and their families that there is not a bad question you can ask."

Team president John Mara, Wellington Mara's eldest son, has a definition and it begins with player names: Lawrence Taylor, Phil Simms, Harry Carson, George Martin, Sam Huff and Andy Robustelli are some of the ones he listed. And then he told Steve Serby of the *New York Post*: "Playing as hard as you can for 60 minutes, and always believing that you can win, no matter what anybody else says."

Corey Webster, a young defensive back, said it was New York Giants Pride that kept him focused when he lost his starting spot and seemed to be losing his place on the team. "My teammates said, 'keep working on your craft,'" he recalled. "Be prepared." Webster maintained focus and pride and it showed in 2007.

"There's no quit in the team," Webster said. "We keep on fighting even if the outcome seems done. We have a belief as a team that we can do it."

There came a time in February 2008 when belief in *New York Giants Pride* brought the team to an achievement no one could have predicted.

– AJP, August, 2008

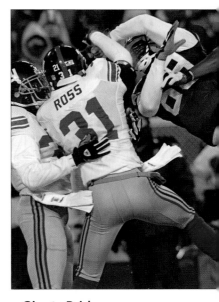

Giants Pride was very much in evidence on both sides of the ball throughout the 2007 season.

Prologue

THE DRIVE BEGINS WITH 2 MINUTES 39 SECONDS TO PLAY IN SUPER BOWL XLII. The New York Giants have the ball at their own 17-yard line, trailing 14-10, and need to play better than these Giants ever have. The biggest audience for a Super Bowl watches in living rooms and bars—and in rec rooms at Camp Victory in Baghdad. At the University of Phoenix Stadium in Glendale, Arizona, 72,000 people lean forward knowing that the end is near. Will the New England Patriots complete a 19–0 season, a record never before accomplished? Or will the Giants—*can* the Giants—somehow complete the upset of the ages?

On the field, one thing the underdog Giants have going for them is the uniform they wear: white with red trim, red numerals, and those brilliant Giant Blue helmets with the neat little **ny** logo on the sides. The white uniform means that they are the visiting team, and this group has remarkably won 10 straight road games, setting an NFL single-season record, bringing them to this stadium on this evening.

In the stands is the Giants' General Manager emeritus Ernie Accorsi who a few minutes

Quarterback Eli Manning's leadership and poise were tested during the late-game drive that decided Super Bowl XLII. On an earlier series in the fourth quarter, an incomplete pass to Plaxico Burress, below, threatened the Giants ability to maintain possession and hold their narrow lead.

earlier heard it from a fan when Eli Manning and Plaxico Burress fail to connect on what seemed a wide-open pass opportunity with 8 minutes 24 seconds to play and the Giants ahead by 3 ("Your quarterback just cost us a championship!"). But Accorsi knows that you don't win—or lose—a three-point game with 8:24 to go. He did not make the trade he made at the 2004 draft to get a quarterback who loses (or seems to win) games with 8:24 to go. He made it to get a quarterback who wins games starting with 2:39 to go.

So when the Giants begin this drive, Accorsi knows it is Eli's time.

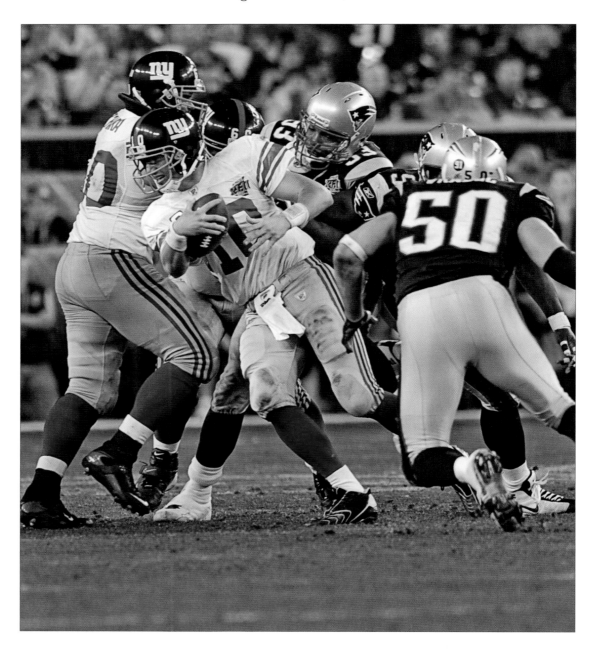

He turns to his son, speaks a few words about the quarterback and then, using his Blackberry, repeats the message to writer Tom Callahan, who is watching at home and who collaborated with Accorsi on the book *The GM*: "If he's going to be what we thought he was going to be, he does it now."

As the Giants are about to take the field for this decisive drive, Shaun O'Hara, the center on offense and an intellectual center of the team, hears Manning telling each teammate: "this is what we play for."

The fans at home worry. Eric Kennedy, founder of the Internet site BigBlue Interactive.com, murmurs, "Please, don't let us lose a game where we held them to 14 points."

On the field, Eli's teammates listen to him. Fourth and one from the 37. Brandon Jacobs for 2.

Three plays later, Manning is about to be tackled for a devastating loss. But he squirts like a watermelon seed from the mass of bodies and spots David Tyree. He spirals the ball to him some 40 yards away. At the top of his leap, Tyree makes the catch. His left hand is immediately yanked away. But he somehow maintains control of the ball between his right hand and his Giant Blue helmet as he heads to the ground.

At his TV, Jay Rosenstein, a fan of more than 50 years, channels the late announcer Jack Buck and shouts: "I don't believe what I just saw!"

Later, David Tyree recalled the play just "slowing down" as it unfolded.

In the NFL control room high above the field, the ambient noise microphone tells the story. "After Tyree's catch," says NFL Senior VP Events Frank Supovitz, who runs that room, "you could hear the buzz pick up. You could hear the excitement."

On third and 11 Steve Smith makes a catch-and-run for 12 yards and a first down. He steps out of bounds to stop the clock, and here we are: first and 10 from the 13.

The play that will be talked about for years to come began with Eli Manning, opposite, scrambling for his life before spotting David Tyree who outjumps and then outwrestles Patriots defender Rodney Harrison to maintain possession.

Thirty-nine seconds to play and for millions of fans around the world the possibility is there, is here—something that the men in Giant Blue helmets have known all along: the Giants can win this game.

In the radio booth, former Giant great, defensive back Dick Lynch, the longtime color analyst, says: "Don't forget Burress has been able to get behind these fellas. Let's see what happens."

In the huddle, Eli calls the play—"62 Café." The team breaks the huddle. There is no shouting, no nerves. The men on both sides of the ball are trained for this moment, pray for this moment, live for this moment. The "I-can't-look" fear, the tight stomachs, the damp palms – these are for the fans in the stands and in the bars of Manhattan… and at the Super Bowl parties around the country and the world… and for those sitting alone because they are too nervous to watch with anyone.

The men on the field know what they are doing. For everyone else, it is a mystery.

As he scans the defense, Eli likes what he sees. Split out from him, 15 yards away, Plaxico Burress likes it, too. The Patriots are going to blitz, trying to stop this relentless drive any way they can. And that means Burress should be facing just one defender, the cornerback Victor Hobbs. Earlier in the game, before it seemed to almost anyone that the Giants could win, Plax had seen the same setup and had come back to the huddle to tell Eli, "I can beat this guy."

"Not now," Eli had decided.

But with the game in the balance, he sees the corner blitz about to come—he thinks "Now." And as he calls signals in that fidgety, don't-let-anyone-get-settled Manning way, he makes certain his blockers know their assignments and that Plax knows the time is "now."

O'Hara snaps the ball from the shotgun. Eli takes it, glances toward the center of the end zone, and then looks to the corner. The Patriots are blitzing but have not reached him. As the quarterback and receiver have anticipated, Plax is one-on-one with Victor Hobbs and begins to run a slant—no it's a fake slant. Hobbs takes the bait. He does not know that the last play Eli and Plax practiced in warm-ups that afternoon was the fake slant and the high fade to the corner. And here it is, the last play.

Eli releases the ball – not a tight, hard spiral, just a soft toss into the lights, into the dome-enclosed atmosphere where traces of smoke from the halftime show remain. And about 30 yards away, Plax looks up and the ball is in the air. "Forever," Manning says.

On the sidelines and in the radio booth and in the stands... and in the living rooms and bars... and the TV rooms and the rec room of Camp Victory... the focus is on one thing.

The ball is in the air and the game is about to be won—or lost. The quarterback is about to affirm what he is or isn't; the Coach is about to realize—or not—that his career is on a new road to distinction. The injured wide receiver who cried earlier in the week because he thought he would miss this chance, turns toward the ball, alone in the end zone.

The ball is in the air and the end of this improbable journey is near. This journey that began in the tumultuous final days of the last season, and has continued through the remarkable events of this one, is almost over. All the hopes and dreams, failures and successes, the laughs and tears on this odyssey, hang suspended on that soft toss.

The ball is in the air. . . .

Giants fans at Super Bowl XLII in Arizona hope for history to three-peat.

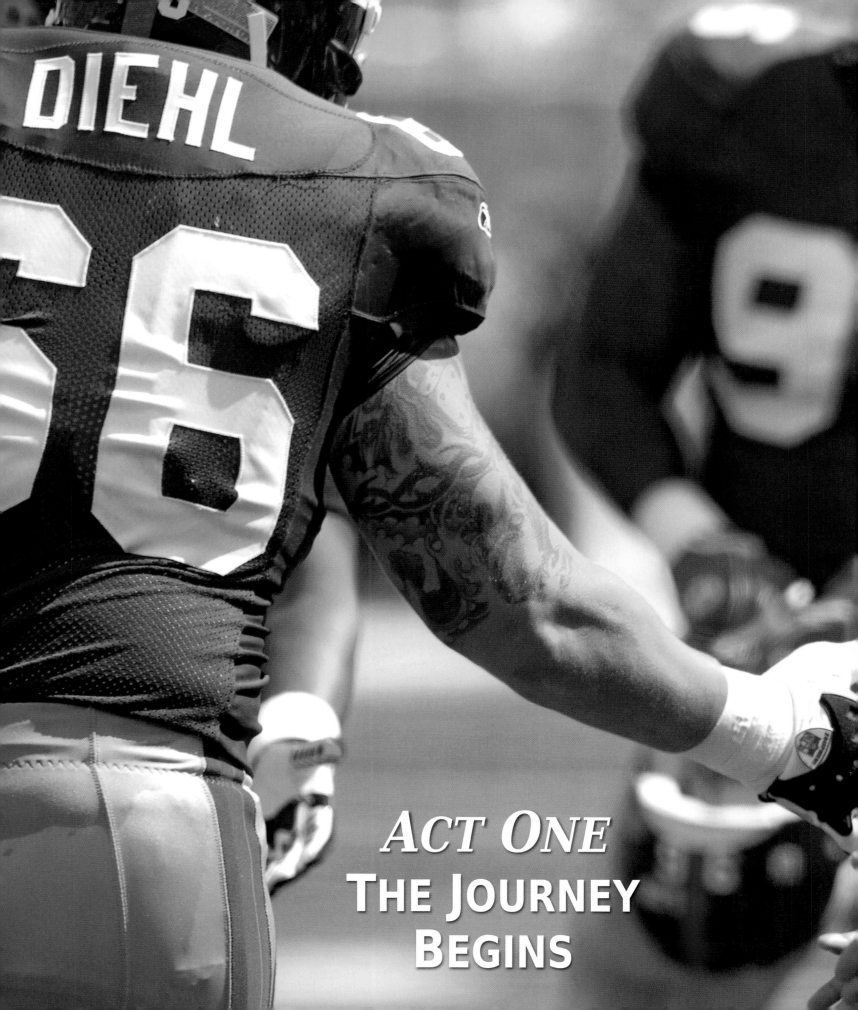

ACT ONE
THE JOURNEY
BEGINS

SCENE ONE
TWO STUMBLES AND A STAND

THIS ODYSSEY STARTS SOMETIME AFTER A FIELD GOAL with no time left on the clock eliminated the troubled and troubling New York Giants from the 2006 NFL playoffs.

The off-season is one of change, but the fan wonders in what direction. The club's premier running back went through with retirement, announced so disruptively in the midst of the 2006 season. The General Manager retired as planned. The Coach returned to the surprise of some, the disapproval of others. The new GM made no moves that seemed to matter and the veteran defensive end contemplated retirement. The quarterback was still the quarterback.

Coach Tom Coughlin revamped his approach to communicating with his players

The first clue to the new direction is the announcement a month after the end of the previous season that GM Jerry Reese has cut the team's ties to veterans Luke Pettigout, Carlos Emmons and LaVar Arrington. That spring's draft produces eight picks but no apparent standouts. The only free agent signed is a linebacker from the Chiefs named Kawika Mitchell, whose primary assets are good health and youth. None of this makes for positive anticipation among the fans. That would change.

The 2007 schedule evokes a consensus that the year will not be easy, beginning with the Cowboys in Dallas on the season's first Sunday night. Many experts have Dallas pegged to reach Super Bowl XLII, while the Giants remain a team that had struggled through injury and uncertainty to finish 2006 at 8-8 and reach the playoffs only after a record-setting night from the now retired running back Tiki Barber.

By the time the players start training camp in Albany, nagging questions remain: Is Eli Manning talented enough to win consistently? Who will replace Barber? What is the impact on the team of Michael Strahan's ambivalence about playing? Will help come from players acquired by trade or through the draft and how will David Diehl do at the vital left tackle position?

Still, there is reason for optimism. Detail-oriented coach Tom Coughlin has formed a leadership council of ten players to offer advice and counsel. Rotating captains? It didn't work last year, the council says, and so before the season begins five permanent captains are picked: Eli Manning, Shaun O'Hara, Jeff Feagles, Antonio Pierce and Michael Strahan who finally decided to play. During camp, one night's team meeting is cancelled so Coughlin can take his men bowling.

From the comfort of a TV studio, Barber criticizes his former quarterback, questioning his leadership. Eli responds:

"I'm not going to lose any sleep about what Tiki has to say. I guess I could have questioned his leadership skills last year, his calling out the coach and [discussing his retirement] in the middle of the season… that

Michael Strahan ended his holdout, became one of the Giants five captains and resumed his role as a leader of the defense.

Rookie of the Year
Jerry Reese, GM

ON JANUARY 16, 2007, GIANTS MANAGEMENT made an announcement that would have an enormous impact on the next season and seasons to come: Jerry Reese was introduced as the new Senior Vice President and General Manager. Reese, who joined the Giants scouting department in 1994, had worked in the front office since 1997 and, in 2002, was named player personnel director by GM Ernie Accorsi. Reese became the third African-American NFL general manager when he succeeded Accorsi.

After introductions at a press conference Reese said: "I would be silly to think I'd be sitting here without God's favor, so I just want everyone to know that I'm a spiritual person and I appreciate the favor that God has given me to be here." Then he thanked the team's owners, the Mara family, and the Tisch family and Accorsi. The next tip of the hat was to the scouts, the guys "who do all the hard work."

Team president John Mara answered the first question: would anyone replace Reese as personnel director?

"Jerry will run the draft this year," Mara said, "just as he has done in previous years."

Some time later, reflecting on the draft process Reese said: "It's not a science; it's not a crapshoot, either." What he meant is that hard work from the scouts results in the picks he makes; hard work by the coaches turns those picks into NFL players. But not every pick pans out.

At that first draft the team made eight selections—cornerback Aaron Ross of Texas, wide receiver Steve Smith of USC, defensive tackle Jay Alford of Penn State, linebacker Zak DeOssie of Brown, tight end Kevin Boss of Western Oregon, tackle Adam Koets of Oregon State, defensive back Michael Johnson of Arizona, and running back Ahmad Bradshaw of Marshall. And it quickly became apparent that they would have an impact.

Asked for the qualities he looked for in a Giants draft pick, Reese said: "Size, speed, smarts—and they have to like to play football."

Reese, who grew up in tiny Tiptonville, Tennessee, and played college football at Tennessee-Martin, got into coaching as soon as he graduated. He understood the meaning that his new job (begun on Martin Luther King Day 2007) could have for other African-Americans.

"It has been a struggle and it is still a struggle in some phases of this business," Reese said. "But I got a shot, and if I can do well, I think it will show other team owners that, 'You know what, look at Jerry Reese.' But it could be corporate America anywhere, someone saying, 'Jerry has been successful, why can't somebody else of color be successful?'"

he's lost the heart. It's tough as a quarterback to read that your running back's lost heart in playing the game and it's the tenth week."

Then he smiles a bit and says: "I'm just happy for Tiki that he's making a smooth transition to the media."

And his teammates love it. He is becoming theirs and they are becoming his.

What is going on here? An outspoken quarterback and a kinder gentler coach. If all this isn't enough, we learn that earlier in the summer, the players and coaches took part in a casino night, organized by Coach during mini-camp.

Coughlin has an answer: "My whole thing is just try to do whatever it is we can to enhance communication and to make sure that we are all on the same page—and that our voice is one and that everybody understands what we are doing and why we are doing it."

Maybe it is a phone call Tom Coughlin gets from former Yankee Manager Joe Torre; maybe it is his family telling him they didn't recognize him as he tore routinely up and down the sidelines shouting and waving wildly; maybe it is Coughlin realizing that he is, in his words, a dinosaur but one who could change.

Or maybe it's that the 61-year-old coach fears that his chosen profession can be taken from him without accomplishing the only goal that matters.

For Eli, maybe it's just time to say "enough" to his critics and those who expect things without reason. Maybe he finally feels comfortable in his fourth NFL season. Whatever it is—surely it is a combination of things that accounts for this new sense of purpose—changed men are running this team.

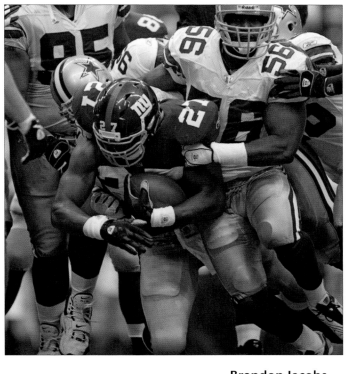

Brandon Jacobs grinds out yards against the Cowboys defense.

One of the key axioms of professional sports is that you have to play the games. Seems simple. You can't whine about the challenge, you can't make excuses over it. Here's your schedule: go play. It's simple, although not everyone sees it that way. But the pros do.

For the 2007 Giants the schedule says the Cowboys in Dallas in game one then the Packers and Brett Favre at Giants Stadium in game two. The reason for optimism in the home opener is that the Pack was 8-8 in 2006 and Brett Favre isn't really Brett Favre anymore. Or is he?

Next, off to Washington for game three, meaning that the season opens against three old-line NFL teams—teams with whom the Giants have histories (the Cowboys and Redskins, opponents twice a year for forever, the Packers, less frequent but longer time rivals).

Substitute running back **Derrick Ward**, above and opposite, rushes for 89 yards and catches four passes against the Cowboys.

September 9, 2007, in Dallas

Up first the Cowboys at Dallas on NBC Sunday Night Football with their red-hot QB Tony Romo, their big-play, big-mouth wide receiver Terrell Owens, and their new coach Wade Phillips who after the team's tumultuous 2006 season replaced ex-Giant coach Bill Parcells.

Tough game.

By the time it is over, linebacker Antonio Pierce has this to say: "We gave up too many big plays and our tackling was horrible. Guys have to step up. We have to get a better rush. At the same time, the secondary and linebackers have to cover tighter. Our offense did a great job moving the ball. But we couldn't come up with that key third down."

Interestingly Pierce speaks like a captain—no "I", just "we". Good or bad, a team has to have that attitude.

Manning is mostly brilliant with four touchdowns and 312 yards passing. The backs have 124 yards rushing but as Pierce says, the defense couldn't stop anything. Plaxico Burress, playing hurt and without practice, has three touchdowns (and 8 catches) and Derrick Ward fills in at running back and runs wild. Some of the eight rookies on the opening roster make big contributions, including wide receiver Steve

Despite pressure from the Dallas defense, **Eli Manning** threw four touchdown passes, three of which were hauled in by **Plaxico Burress**, opposite.

Smith has three catches.

But the Cowboys make 12 plays of 15 yards or more. They gain 478 yards, and hold off a late Giants rally. Worst of all, they leave Eli Manning with a shoulder injury, running back Brandon Jacobs and defensive end Osi Umenyiora with knee injuries, and cornerback Kevin Dockery with a bad ankle. Not exactly what anyone had in mind.

Still there was all that offense and the defense was sure to get better. And maybe Eli would only miss a game or two.

"It's frustrating, because we work hard," Pierce said. "We went out the first time on Sunday night with everybody watching and we didn't rise to the occasion."

COWBOYS 45 • GIANTS 35 • (0-1)

A season ruined by injury in 2006 seems to have started right back up in 2007. RB Brandon Jacobs, 260 pounds of speed, smarts and muscle—and in the hot lights of replacing the departed Tiki—has a sprained knee ligament. He is no longer the one-yard-for-the-touchdown back that he was in the past but the featured guy, and now he's injured. And the quarterback lands on his shoulder and has to leave for a play in favor of the 290-pound untested backup Jared Lorenzen. But Manning returns. He is surely not right but he's there. He'll miss the next game it is assumed. "I know the best thing that you can do is be in the training room, get all of the treatment you can and try to get as much rest and do everything possible to get healthy," says the quarterback. "So that's what I'll do."

As for Umenyiora, he is probable…

Going into the Packers game, the home opener, no one can be as optimistic as they might hope.

Coach Coughlin says: "I am not discouraged about anything. Like I said, I am disappointed in our first game but not discouraged."

But as the week goes on and player-availability questions remain unanswered, Coughlin says: "There is no comfort. I don't have any comfort. What's comfortable?"

Home opener versus Green Bay. Wide receiver **Sinorice Moss** (83) responds to the crowd.

ABSOLUTELY
NO
SMOKING, GUM,
SUN FLOWER SEEDS,
FOOD OR BEVERAGE
ON THE FIELD

ZERO TOLERANCE

Lawrence Tynes's 48-yard field goal, right, capped an eight-play 41-yard drive and gave the Giants a 10-7 lead late in the first quarter.

September 16, 2007, at Giants Stadium vs. Green Bay

If you love football the season seems too short. It starts when the weather is warm, the sun still direct, the leaves on the trees—it is summer. But in a flash it's late December, the leaves are gone, daylight is fleeting, and the games are about to end. Still the season is long enough to overcome a bad day or two at the beginning. A strong mid-season can compensate for early or late stumbles. It's not a play, a series, a quarter, a half, or even a game. It's a season and it takes time; a marathon, not a sprint.

As the Giants open their home schedule, the fans and players at Giants Stadium are graced by a visit from former Giant defensive end, George Martin, a hero of Super Bowl XXI and about to become a hero of another sort. Martin is beginning a walking journey of 3,000 miles across the country. His goal: to raise millions of dollars for health care for 9/11 rescue workers. In this and so many ways, the Big Blue stays connected to its past, to its players, great and not so great. Martin's presence brings 38 other former Giants onto the field at halftime to hold an American flag in the shape of the United States as the team honors the sixth anniversary of the attacks of 2001.

It is a warm, beautiful afternoon, and hopes for the home opener are boosted by the presence on the field in warm-ups of the starting quarterback.

And in the first half, those hopes are rewarded as the Giants take a 10-7 lead on a Manning-to-Burress touchdown and a Lawrence Tynes field goal.

But in the third quarter Brett Favre completes all 11 of his passes, including two for touchdowns. The Giants stop moving the ball as penalties stall drives and possible touchdowns turn into field goal attempts. By the fourth quarter the fans have seen enough. With many

Giant Among Giants
George Martin

WHEN GEORGE MARTIN VISITED GIANTS STADIUM on September 16, 2007 he came as a star of Giants teams of the '70s and '80s. He arrived after the first few miles of his walk across America, which had begun nearby that day at the George Washington Bridge.

He left to become a hero to millions.

This was no mere walking tour George Martin was on—it was a 3000-mile-plus mission to raise funds for the care and treatment of the first responders to the tragedy of September 11, 2001—and to spread the message of their need. Here he was, six years later, doing something about it.

Despite some brutal weather—winter cold and searing heat—he reached the Pacific on June 21, 2008, arriving in San Diego, where he was met by many of those first responders he was walking for. He had raised millions.

"You could write books about the generosity of the people we saw," Martin said. "One guy pulled up alongside of us on the road and said he'd heard about the walk on the radio and he wanted to contribute. So he gave me $20. Then he drove off. A few hours later, there he was pulling alongside and saying, 'I should have been more generous before.' And he pulled out $200 this time."

The Giants contributed more than $40,000 to the effort and some priceless exposure when Martin appeared on the field at halftime of the Green Bay game. He was joined by 38 former Giants of the last 50 years. They carried an American flag in the shape of the United States.

"Wellington Mara said there's no such thing as an ex-Giant," said Martin, a veteran of 14 NFL seasons. "There's just active Giants and inactive Giants." And Giants who are giants, like George Martin.

parking spots out of commission due to construction of the new stadium, a fourth-quarter deficit of 28-13 has fans heading for exits. The traffic jam on the way out is not what fans had expected, and memories of last season's collapse and the doubts of the offseason are heightened.

One lifelong fan, a New York attorney named Bob Schrager, who has quietly enjoyed the Giants for more than 30 years, sits in the fading sunshine and bellows: "Bye, bye Tommy." More quietly, he mutters his belief that the team has quit on Coughlin.

Another longtime fan, Marc Zwerdling, a New Englander who grew up on the New York side of the dividing line between Giant fan and Patriot fan—Yankee fan and Red Sox fan—sees a bright side: "At least Eli was healthy."

Brett Favre completed 29 of 38 passes for 286 yards and three touchdowns as the Packers dominated at the Meadowlands.

Coughlin, having expected much more, says: "I think we're a better football team than we have shown. Obviously, I don't have any real grounds for saying that; it's just a belief. I do believe we are all in it together, and I do believe that we are all embarrassed."

And the Giants are 0-2 for the first time since 1996.

PACKERS 35 • GIANTS 13 • (0-2)

Defensive coordinator **Steve Spagnuolo** hangs tough after an 0-2 start.

"We're not going to get any worse, that I can promise," defensive end Osi Umenyiora says before the trip to Washington for game three. "I'm not necessarily guaranteeing we're going to win the game, but I guarantee we're going to play better."

This sentiment is echoed in an peculiar way by a howling air horn belonging to Antonio Pierce, which he blasts in the locker room as a presumed joke after several days of not talking at all. When he is asked about the defense and its troubles, he responds with the air horn. Funny, he thinks, and a way to deflect attention from the difficult first two games.

But it isn't funny and rather than deflecting attention it magnifies the problem and makes many think that the locker room is turning as dysfunctional as it had been in 2006. It gets Pierce a radio scolding from Tiki Barber and Shannon Sharpe, which means nothing to Pierce, and a more private rebuke from Coach Coughlin and team management, which means a lot. Pierce says he was trying to have fun but he apologizes "for scaring everybody."

And so it goes. An 0-2 team with some questionable locker room behavior has to go on the road to play the improved Washington Redskins. If there's reason for hope, it is this: last year, the Giants needed—and got—a victory at FedEx Field in their final regular-season game to end their slump and make the playoffs.

Still, the team is 0-2, they've given up 80 points and scored 48. And the new Defensive Coordinator is facing questions. "You can't let two games shake your confidence in a 16-game season," says Steve Spagnuolo. "When you're in certain adverse situations, you rely on prior experience. In 2000 and, I think, '03 or '02, we [in Philadelphia] began 0-2. And we ended up in the NFC Championship Game. So it's not shaken me yet.

"If you classify it as 'tough,' I think this business is tough period. I think it's tough when you are winning, I think it is tough when you are shutting people out. So to me it is not toughness, it is the process. Continue to do what you believe in. That's what we are going to stick to."

Optimism endures. Just the fact that Spagnuolo is talking to the media, and in turn to fans, is refreshing. Previous coordinators rarely spoke to the media, but a league mandate has changed that. And for some reason Spagnuolo's speaking is in itself a boost to fan confidence.

The Giants' Hero
Lt. Col. Greg Gadson

LT. COL. GREG GADSON'S EFFECT ON THE NEW YORK Giants' 2007 season could not be anticipated—his impact could not be measured. Gadson is a graduate of West Point, where he played football for Army. On his last tour of duty in Iraq, Gadson's vehicle hit a roadside bomb, and he was severely injured. Both of his legs were amputated.

During his recovery and rehabilitation in late June he got a visit at Walter Reed Hospital from Mike Sullivan, his former Army teammate, now an assistant coach in charge of wide receivers for the Giants. He came with gifts for his injured comrade—an autographed Giants helmet and hat.

"I've got a friend who's hurt," was all Sullivan told the players about why they were signing the helmet and hat.

At the end of Sullivan's visit, Gadson recalled, "I told him I'd like to see the game when the team plays here in September."

After the Giants got off to its 0-2 start, Sullivan approached Coach Coughlin with the idea that his friend might be a good speaker on the night before the coming Redskins game. Soon Gadson was on the phone with Coach Coughlin, who invited him to address the team.

Now the question was: what to say.

"I wanted to talk about opportunities and responsibilities," said Gadson. "Maybe I can help them reach their goals. I didn't want to let Mike Sullivan down. I didn't want the Coach saying: 'Sullivan, why'd you bring this guy in here?'"

Not much chance of that.

On Saturday night at the Giants' downtown Washington hotel, all meetings were cancelled. "Only Coach and Mike knew I was going to be talking," Gadson said. "I got some strange looks when the players came into the room."

Coach Coughlin talked for a few minutes and then he introduced his guest.

Gadson talked about teamwork and team-building, about sacrifice and commitment, about loving the guys you are working with. As pro football players, they'd heard a lot of it already, but never from such a source.

The next day's score at halftime, 17-3 Redskins, seemed to indicate that the Giants' struggles would go on. But "I thought if these guys keep their poise," said Gadson, " they're going to come out all right."

The result that day: Giants 24, Redskins 17, and a winning streak had begun.

OK, we the fans are optimistic. But a fan's optimism is endemic. Why are the players and coaches optimistic?

In part, it has to do with a visit the night before the game from Lt. Col. Greg Gadson of the U.S. Army, a college teammate at West Point of Giants' assistant coach Mike Sullivan. Gadson, who wore No. 98 at Army, the same number worn in college by the Giants great linebacker Lawrence Taylor, lost both legs after his vehicle was hit by a roadside bomb in Iraq the previous May. He is recuperating and rehabilitating at Walter Reed when he gets a visit from his old teammate Sullivan.

Sullivan tells his boss about his friend and Coach invites Gadson to address the team at their hotel on Saturday night.

"One of the things I told the team is I love football," Gadson says soon afterwards. "It's been a big part of my life and it still is from the standpoint of how I am fighting through what I am going through now and how I lived in the Army.

"I don't want anyone to misconstrue that football is like combat," Gadson said. "What I told the team is that it's the same type of emotional investment. These kinds of things demand your all. It's about team. Team is selfless."

Coach thinks a message from Gadson will do his team good. "I wanted the team to hear from a real hero," he says. "We can learn so many things about a person who has been through an extremely difficult part of his life."

Even the opposing coach, Washington's Hall-of-Famer Joe Gibbs, expects more from the Giants. "All of us know the Giants," he says. "First of all, that team beat us twice last year with most of the same players. You can imagine how hard they're going to play. Right now they're sitting there at 0-2—a real, real good football team. I know what we're going to get."

Pressure by the Giants defense resulted in four fumbles by Washington quarterback **Jason Campbell**.

September 23, 2007, in Washington

The first half is as bad as or worse than the previous two games. A turnover and a long drive lead to touchdowns by Redskins Clinton Portis and Chris Cooley, giving Washington a 17-3 lead at the half to the delight of 90,000 fans.

Back home, some fans spend halftime thinking about who the Giants should draft to take over at quarterback. Brian Brohm of Louisville is a name tossed around. Or what about a running back like Darren McFadden of Arkansas? It goes without saying that many expect to be rooting for a different coach pretty soon.

The team, however, spends halftime refocusing, and in the second half Manning and Burress connect on five passes and a touchdown. Derrick Ward, filling in for Jacobs, runs for 47 yards, same as he had in the first half.

"What I really liked was that our offense gave the opponent ten points, OK?" Coughlin would say. "Our defense never got down. The defense is in the locker room encouraging the offense at half-time. The offense is encouraging each other. The offensive players are encouraging Plaxico, and the special teams guys are getting there... So even though the score was 17-3, everybody in the locker room was pretty convinced that if we take the ball and score we would be one score down and we would be in a position to be in the game again."

When the Redskins get the ball with 2:17 to play following a punt return to the Giants' 35, the Giants are not only in it but leading 24-17. On third and 21, the Redskins gain 18, and, following a Washington penalty, pick up 15 on fourth down. Three plays later Jason Campbell's pass to Antwaan Randle El gives Washington a first down on the one.

Reuben Droughns had three carries for three yards and two touchdowns.

A spike stops the clock and Washington has three downs and 51 seconds to get in the end zone.

"We knew what was at stake, especially the leadership in that huddle," says defensive end Justin Tuck, who moves to tackle in the goal-line defense. "A.P. [Pierce] is screaming, Stray [Michael Strahan] is screaming, Osi is screaming. We were saying, 'We are not going to lose this football game no matter if they get to the inch line. They still have to cross that white and if they don't cross that white we win.'"

The Redskins never do cross it. On second down Campbell throws incomplete, on third Ladell Betts runs to the left side and appears to have a lane before he is stopped by Kawika Mitchell—the "only" free agent GM Jerry Reese signed, remember?

"I was just doing my job," Mitchell says. "I was the one that was supposed to make the tackle and I made it. It is as simple as that."

Fourth down. Umenyiora and Tuck on the right side of the D Line feel the play will go their way.

"Of course they were going to," Umenyiora says. "Where else were they going to go?"

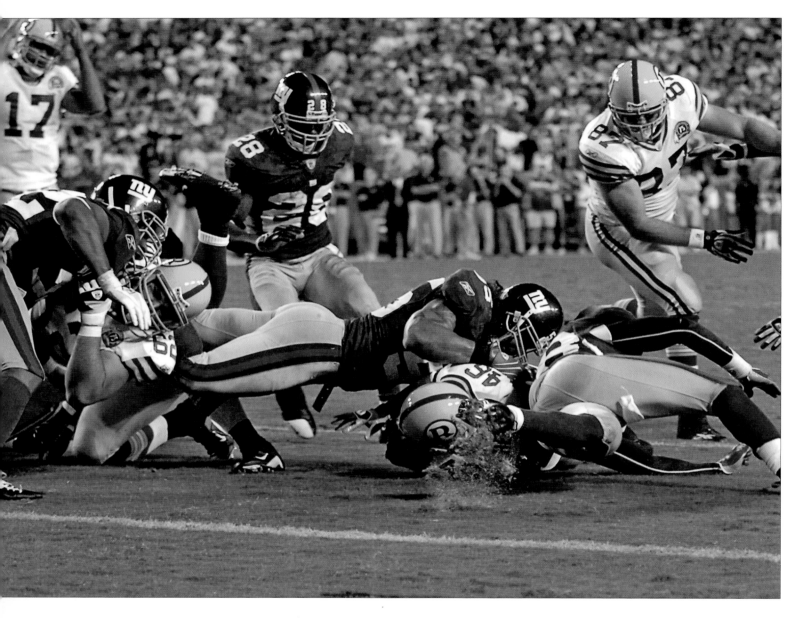

This key fourth-down stop sealed the Gaints' first win.

And sure enough, Betts runs their way. But Umenyiora and Tuck get penetration and rookie cornerback Aaron Ross shoots through and cuts down Betts to secure the Giants' victory. The official play-by-play has James Butler making that tackle but it is Ross. Time to start paying attention to these rookies.

When it is over, a game ball goes to Lt. Col. Greg Gadson.

GIANTS 24 • REDSKINS 17 • (1-2)

By a distance not much greater than the length of this page, the season has turned.

SCENE TWO
THE STREAK

THE 1-2 TEAM IS SHOWING SIGNS OF LIFE, particularly on offense, despite the injuries to the No. 1 running back and the No. 1 receiver. Derrick Ward, considered by few if anyone to be a replacement for Barber, has 273 yards on the ground in the three games, as Brandon Jacobs remains sidelined with his knee injury.

Donovan McNabb feels the heat from **Osi Umeyioria's** pass rush. The Giants would sack the Eagles' quarterback 12 times for a combined loss of 62 yards. Umeyioria would be credited with six.

"I was just sitting back letting things progress," Ward said. "I knew what I could do. I knew I could play in the NFL, and I knew that it was going to take patience. I was going to get my chance. It was just a matter of when."

The ankle injury to receiver Plaxico Burress keeps him from practice but not games. He has 15 catches and five touchdowns.

"It's really frustrating, because I really want to get out there and practice," Burress says. "That's what really makes me feel more comfortable going into the game on Sunday. I'm going into the games now a little more nervous and with a little more butterflies. But I think I've been playing long enough to go into a game under-standing where I need to be."

Try to imagine a pre-2007 Tom Coughlin being willing to have a player who can't practice but manages to play in the games each week. His faith in Burress to do the work needed to get ready is revealing. "We've juggled this from

The Eagles were landed: **Michael Strahan** played his part in the sack attack.

the beginning of training camp, " says Coughlin. "It is frustrating. It is frustrating for Plax. But his heart is in the right place. He wants to play. He wants to help his team. So we're going to try to do the very best we can, knowing full well that he is not going to get many reps. He has a lot of pride. He will know all of the assignments."

September 30, 2007, in Giants Stadium vs. Philadelphia

This is the second appearance on Sunday Night Football for the Giants, and it is their first meeting with the Eagles, completing a four-game NFC gauntlet.

For all the good news and good numbers coming from the offense, the defense is still under review.

Until tonight.

Playing one of the great games in Giants history, the defense ties a league record with 12 sacks, six of them by Osi Umenyiora -- his first sacks of the season and a team record. The festival starts early and goes all night.

"Sacks come in bunches," says Umenyiora, clearly recovered from his first-game injury. "As long as you keep working, as long as you keep putting pressure on the quarterback, it's eventually going to happen for you."

Osi is of course being modest. Hard work and pressure will surely pay off, but like that? Unlikely.

Strahan's sack of Eagles QB Donovan McNabb in the second quarter puts him ahead of the great Lawrence Taylor, with a Giants career record of 133.5. Taylor, who naturally is watching from the sidelines, waves a finger at Strahan and later, in a good-natured dig, adds: "I want to congratulate Michael on setting the new official career sack record for the Giants. And I want to remind him that I had nine-and-a-half sacks [as a rookie in 1981], before they even started counting them. So he has some more work to do."

"I could have 500 sacks," Strahan says, "but that does not make me another LT."

Burress has four more receptions and the only offensive TD, and Ward runs for another 80 yards.

With all their sacks—and Kawika Mitchell's touchdown a fumble recovery—the defense makes this night happen. For the Giants, that's always the way things work best.

GIANTS 16 • EAGLES 3 • (2-2)

Next up is the team that should be a natural rival but really isn't, the Jets. The level of anticipation for a "visit" from the Jets is not close to that before a Cowboys, Redskins or Eagles game. And the Jets, for whom much had truly been expected, are 1-3.

The Giants are bolstered by the return of running back Brandon Jacobs. There is little time given to enjoying the latest success. Coach won't have it. "First of all, I told the players, 'Forget about last week. Last week is over,' says Coughlin. "The best example of what can happen were the Eagles [who had 56 points the week before getting sacked by the Giants]. The simple fact of the matter is that as soon as you can move on to the next opponent, the better off you are."

Teaching is easier when the team wins, he says, so "we started off last week talking about improvement. We gave every player a list of improvements that they personally had to make. And we are really proud and pleased with last week's defensive effort, for example. We saw some things on special teams that were a little bit better. We saw a couple of things on offense that were okay in the first half. But we have a long way to go."

October 7, 2007, in Giants Stadium vs. Jets

What's that sound as the players leave the field at the half? Boos. For the home team. Boos because the Giants are listless all over again. Eli's QB rating is 0.0 and he has 22 yards passing; Burress has no catches, Jeremy Shockey one. Jacobs's second carry ends in a fumble that the Jets return for a touchdown. The Jets lead 17-7 lead at the half.

Last week is last week.

"First half, we played about as poorly as we could," says Manning. "But that's why you have two halves in every game."

The second half is something else again. Manning completes 10 of

A long evening for the **Eagles'** veteran signal caller.

Never Enough
The D-Line

IN HIS LAST DRAFT AS GM OF THE GIANTS, Ernie Accorsi used his first-round pick on Mathias Kiwanuka, a pass-rushing defensive end from Boston College. He did this despite having Pro-Bowl-quality ends in Michael Strahan and Osi Umenyiora and a young prospect named Justin Tuck on the roster. When asked about his thinking, Accorsi said simply, "You never, ever have enough pass rushers." By the 2007 season, that bit of wisdom made Accorsi sound prophetic.

With Strahan and Umenyiora demanding constant attention from offensive linemen on the outside, the tackles Fred Robbins and Barry Cofield clogged the middle and shut down the opposition's running game. The Giants became one of the league's best defenses against the run, and often used Tuck on the inside, which gave new vision to what an interior defensive lineman could be. Tuck used his combination of defensive-tackle size and strength and defensive-end speed and agility to blast through lines and send quarterbacks to the turf 10 times. Kiwanuka had been converted to outside linebacker for 2007, before he went down with a broken leg against the Detroit Lions. But when he was healthy, the Giants often used four pass-rushing defensive ends by sending Kiwanuka back to the line. That left opposing offensive coordinators scratching their heads and opposing quarterbacks holding theirs.

In years past, offensive tackles would get help from guards against Umenyiora and Strahan, but the presence of Tuck and Kiwanuka on the interior of the defensive line forced a change. "They're not able to use their guards on us," Umenyiora told The New York Times after the Washington game. "Because if you do that, you have two very, very good pass rushers that the quarterback has to be worried about."

15 for two touchdowns, one to Shockey, his first of the season, and one to Burress, whose high-stepping, stiff-arming run downfield leaves many in the audience in awe, even if he isn't so impressed. "I just practiced that back in the day when I would see Eric Dickerson do it," Burress says of the stiff arm. "I know if I can get my palm on the crown of their helmet, then they won't be able to get their hands on me."

In the press box, *New York Times* columnist William Rhoden wonders if Burress, and even his coach, are about to become the biggest stars in New York sports. "There's a void on Broadway," Rhoden writes. "For Burress and Coughlin, center stage is there for the taking."

And a new concept turns up (Coughlin's Law?)—when things could go wrong they don't.

Giants rookie No. 1 draft pick Aaron Ross, a talented cornerback from Texas, sits for the first half under a mini-suspension for violating unspecified team rules. ("Between him and me," Coach says.)

"It was a mistake," Ross says. "I feel like I responded really well. Coach didn't treat me like I was out of the game. Every time the defense came to the sideline, I was in there with them getting the plays. I wouldn't say that I was out of the game, I just wasn't in the game out on the field."

In the second half, he's very much in the game, intercepting a pass near the goal-line early in the fourth quarter to stop a Jets drive and then picking another Pennington pass that he returns for a game-clinching touchdown.

Two halves, indeed.

GIANTS 35 • JETS 24 • (3-2)

Sam Madison's 25-yard interception return is one of very few bright spots in a listless first half by the Giants.

Every day it seems there are positive signs for this team. Against the Jets, Brandon Jacobs follows his first quarter fumble with the best rushing day of his career—100 yards. He's the first running back other than Tiki Barber to do that since Ron Dayne seven years earlier. Ward has 54 yards and the running game is going well—sure evidence that the offensive line is an able unit. Find a successful offensive line and you've probably found a successful team.

"They have been very solid, particularly running the ball," says the new offensive coordinator Kevin Gilbride. "They are very physical; they are a very proud group and I think they are one of those groups that the collective is better than the sum of the individual parts. The play well together and they play hard."

The team that started out 0-2 and seemed headed nowhere is now 3-2 and going back on the road to the Georgia Dome, a friendly place in the past.

The team gets three days off from practice before beginning work for the Falcons. A reward? Coughlin is asked. Planned, the coach says.

Amani Toomer became the Giants's career leader in reception with his 587th against the Falcons.

October 15, 2007, in Atlanta

For 10 seasons wide receiver Amani Toomer elevated the Giants offense with his steady productive presence and brought dignity to the locker room with his thoughtful comments and quiet ways. But halfway through his 11th season, 2006, he suffered a devastating knee injury that could have been a career-ender. Surgery to repair his ACL was required. Yet here he is in Atlanta in game six of season 12 about to break some team records, including one that has stood for a remarkably long time. He is no longer the number one target but vital just the same.

"The reason why I had the surgery," Toomer says. "was not because I had to have it, but because I had to remove all doubt and make sure that I could come back and make some big offensive plays for a couple more years."

Tonight against the Falcons Toomer sets the team record for receptions with his final of the night, career catch number 587, passing Tiki Barber. He scores a touchdown, his 48th, which ties him for first on the team list with Kyle Rote, a star of Giants teams in the 50s and 60s.

'It's Time to Win'
Antonio Pierce

WHEN ANTONIO PIERCE SIGNED WITH THE GIANTS in March 2005, Pete Prisco of CBSSportsline.com, wrote: "Pierce is a 26-year-old player on the way up. He played every snap last year for the Redskins at middle linebacker, which means he stays on the field in passing situations. Love this move."

Talking to the media that day, Pierce gave Giants fans another reason to fall in love.

"It's time to win the East," he said. "And knock Philly off."

In Pierce's first season the Giants did win the East, but now in season three, everyone expected more from the former undrafted free agent out of the University of Arizona. Coach Tom Coughlin was one of the first to show confidence in the linebacker in 2007, picking Pierce as one of 10 members of the new team leadership council and naming him one of the team's five permanent captains.

After the Giants lost their first two games and gave up 80 points, Pierce's locker-room stunt, blowing an air horn as the media asked questions, turned into a mini-crisis. Coach and management let Pierce know they expected leadership to take other forms.

"At the time, it was just something to get people off our defense, off our D-coordinator, off our coach," Pierce said. "I didn't mind taking that responsibility."

That week's game ended with the Giants stopping the Redskins on the goal line for their first victory which proved to be the beginning of a six-game winning streak. In the huddle in the fourth quarter no one was louder, no one more insistent that the Redskins would not score, than Pierce.

In total career yards, he passes Frank Gifford to move into second place behind Tiki.

But even the forlorn Falcons manage to take an early lead on the Giants. Then Big Blue scores 24 straight points and wins its seventh straight at the Georgia Dome, which provides a curious (and comfortable) mix of home and road for the team. Given that many Giants players are from the South, and that the team has many fans in the area, or who made the trip, the stadium has the feel of home. And when Derrick Ward scores the final touchdown on a nine-yard run, the familiar voice on the stadium loudspeakers is that of The Boss, New Jersey's own Bruce Springsteen—the song, "Glory Days."

GIANTS 31 • FALCONS 10 • (4-2)

Six sacks took their toll on injury replacement QB **Trent Dilfer.**

Anyone who thought after Week 2 that a question could be posed to Coach about his team being overconfident heading into Week 7, raise your hand. Hmmm.

"I'm very vigilant about those kinds of things," says Coughlin. "What you are trying to do is to force the players to remember that if you are still thinking about yesterday today, then you are not getting a whole lot done today. So it is always going forward. I can't control how much smoke is being blown by the media. I really can't. And yet the same people that were writing four or five weeks ago that we weren't a good team are writing now that we are. But you have to be humble. You have to realize that in every National Football League game there are three or four plays that make the difference."

The next opponent back home is the 49ers whose young QB Alex Smith is injured and will be replaced by Trent Dilfer, a name particularly familiar to the two veterans of Super Bowl XXXV, the recordsetters Strahan and Toomer.

October 21, 2007, in Giants Stadium vs. San Francisco

There are lots of statistics that tell of the Giants' performance on this warm autumn day, but two are the biggest—four turnovers, six sacks. The turnovers, "quick change situations," Coach calls them, put the Giants well ahead in the second quarter—two of them coming on consecutive plays and producing 10 points.

In the third quarter, Osi Umenyiora sacks Dilfer and causes a fumble. He picks it up and runs 75 yards for a touchdown—"our best drive of the game," as center Shaun O'Hara jokingly called the run later.

The pressure from the Giants defense is taking a big toll on the opponents, and the memory of the 80 points scored against the team in its first two games is starting to dim in favor of more pleasant thoughts.

"I'm very aware of our sack pressure and our hits on the quarterback," says Coughlin whose QBs have only been sacked seven times. "We've had games where we didn't sack the quarterback but hit him a few times. Let's face it, in the National Football League the quarterback position is the position that turns the ball over by virtue of either fumble or interceptions. So the more pressure you put on that position, the more chance you have for a turnover. Yes, I am very much aware of that stuff."

The offensive highlights of note were Toomer's 49th touchdown catch for the team record and Brandon Jacobs' 107 yards rushing, another personal best.

Next, "a business trip."

GIANTS 33 • 49ERS 15 • (5-2)

Justin Tuck (91) and Osi Umenyiora (72) enjoying a pleasant day at the office.

No National Football League regular season game has ever been played outside North America until now. So the Giants and Dolphins in London's Wembley Stadium is an event. Coach wants it to be all business, but the players can't completely resist the attractions of their next game site. Cameras catch Sam Madison walking the streets of downtown London, talking to everyone he sees; Amani Toomer walks across Tower Bridge to the Tower of London; Plaxico Burress does a mini-tour with a reporter; and Eli Manning visits No. 10 Downing Street with an autographed No. 10 Manning jersey just in case the Prime Minister doesn't have one.

But the team also gets the message from Coach: "The focus is on Miami, but we need to allow the players to reflect on the historical significance of the game."

October 28, 2007, in Wembley Stadium, London
Giants vs. Miami

So surprising that it's raining in London! But a game in the mud—isn't that one of the reasons we love pro football?

"A soccer pitch is very different than a football field," says NFL Sr. VP of Events Frank Supovitz who handles logistics for the London adventure. "The pitch is cultivated to have the shortest possible grass blades not a lush concentration. It's meant to let the ball roll unimpeded. A football field is lush, thick and long for player traction. Combine the short grass with the size of the players, cleats, the rain, and a recent soccer match, and you have a game played on a slippery muddy surface." Makes it fun to watch but tough to play.

Third-year linebacker **Reggie Torbor** (53), opposite, fights the rain and the Dolphins in London's new Wembley Stadium, shown below.

It Takes a Big Man
Brandon Jacobs

THERE ARE PLENTY OF PLAYERS in the NFL who stand 6-4 and weigh 264, run fast and dole out punishing hits. But very few are carrying the football. Brandon Jacobs is one of those very few and is a big problem for defenses. Former Giants running back Ottis Anderson, a big man in his own right, said of defending against Jacobs: "Your whole approach defensively is how to bring someone that big down."

With the departure of Tiki Barber, Jacobs entered the 2007 season primed to be the featured back. This planned succession was delayed in the opening game in Dallas when Jacobs suffered a knee injury that sidelined him for three games. There were whispers: Is Jacobs too physical to be a featured back? Will he have to alter his style to minimize impact to his body?

When he returned in Week 5 against the Jets, Jacobs had the answers as he ran over, around and through defenders on his way to his first 100-yard game as a pro. Jacobs would run for more than 100 yards in two out of the next three weeks, including a huge day in London, where he gained 131 yards in the mud.

Offensive coordinator Kevin Gilbride was asked if there was a player Jacobs reminded him of.

"Nobody," Gilbride said.

Though most only see his size and strength, Jacobs told the Times' John Branch, "I have a soft side that I like people to see. I'm not mean." And when you see the photos of Jacobs' young son Brayden, which line his Giants Stadium locker, you're not surprised when he says, "They're just so I can see what I'm playing for."

Center **Shaun O'Hara** surveys the opposing D and shares his findings with **Eli**, above. Defensive tackle **Barry Cofield**, opposite, found conditions deteriorating on a muddy field.

With the fans under a roof and a field soaked by rain, the best weapon on offense is the safest, 264 pound Brandon Jacobs. For the third time this season he sets a personal best with 131 yards on 23 carries.

"I've never really had to run in the mud before," Jacobs says. "I did it once in high school, but I'm not really a fan of it. It takes some traction away, and you're not able to move as well. We had to take choppier steps and get what we could. We left a lot of big runs out there, but we kept the chains moving, and that's what's most important."

The offensive line loves it.

"It was getting down and dirty— smashmouth football in the mud," left tackle David Diehl says. "It's like you played when you were a kid, just enjoying the experience."

The second-half kickoff is slightly delayed by the visit of a London streaker. The winless Dolphins score a late touchdown to make it close. The 81,000 fans seem to enjoy themselves.

The first half of the season is done.

GIANTS 13 • DOLPHINS 10 • (6-2)

That's six in a row, if you're not paying close attention. The 0-2 team down 14 points at halftime in game three is now 6-2. And from that halftime in suburban Washington to the end of the game in the muck at Wembley, the score, thank you very much, is Giants 152, the other guys 62. This rarely happens in the National Football League no matter who the opponents are.

How good could this get?

ACT TWO
THE TEMPEST

THE PLAYERS SCRAPE OFF THE MUD AND HEAD HOME. Surely no one on the airplane thinks much has been accomplished. But Coach is pleased. "Our team has earned the right to be in the position we're in," he says. "We've done many, many good things along the way."

As players scatter for the bye week, Brandon Jacobs is named NFC Offensive Player of the Month, having returned from his injury with three 100-yard rushing games and 424 yards overall. Most of the team's numbers are good: fewer penalties, longer possession times, better rushing totals, fewer sacks allowed.

"Six-and-two is a great start," says Amani Toomer, "but we are not going to rest on where we are."

When the team returns to practice there is a surprise participant, No. 17 Plaxico Burress. "All my teammates started clapping," he says about his first practice catch since September 12.

"The team gave him a Bronx cheer," jokes Coach Coughlin, who had obviously heard something different.

Last season, like this one, produced six victories in eight games. But in '06 you couldn't be as excited for the second half with so many players injured. In 2007, the lineup is intact.

"By and large we are going to present a stronger team than last year,"

Coughlin says about the half-season to come.

Running back Brandon Jacobs submits a note of caution: "Last year we were satisfied and we got our butts beat," he tells the press. "No one in this locker room is satisfied about anything."

"'Run the race against yourself.' We use that phrase continually," says Coughlin. "The race is not against the guy in the next lane. How good can you be? And we use the symbol 'Three to one.' That's all three phases—offense, defense and special teams—playing as one and playing their best. It hasn't happened yet. The thing I've said a lot this week is, 'Now.' N-O-W. Now.'"

That sounds more like the demanding coach we know.

Sam Madison (29) and Gibril Wilson (28) ride Terrell Owens out of bounds. Owens would have 25- and 50-yard TD receptions in this game. Kawika Mitchell, opposite, brings down Dallas running back Julius Jones.

November 11, 2007, in Giants Stadium vs. Dallas

The 7-1 Cowboys won the opener against the Giants and, with a victory, can almost clinch the East Division. While a Cowboy victory would put the Giants just two games behind, they would, because of the tie-breaking procedure, need three wins more than the Cowboys during the latter part of the season to pass them. A Giants victory will bring the teams even. This is a two-game game.

The first half has the feel of the first game; no one's doing very much stopping of anyone. A Giants field goal at the end of the half ties the score at 17-17 and provides a reason for optimism that lasts only briefly.

On the first Cowboy possession of the second half, their drive seems about to stall three times on successive third downs. And three times it doesn't (Julius Jones runs for 10 on third and 2; Tony Romo to Patrick

Jeremy Shockey caught a career-high 12 passes for 129 yards.

Crayton for 15 on third and 7; Romo to Crayton for 13 on third and 11). And then it's Romo to Terrell Owens for 25 yards and a TD.

Quickly the Giants seem to regain momentum on a kick return by the rookie Ahmad Bradshaw to the Cowboy 2. But wait, there's a flag back downfield. Rookie tight end Kevin Boss has been caught holding and the play comes back, First and 10 on the Giant 17 instead of first and goal. The team regroups, and the drive takes it to the 6, from where Jacobs bulls into the end zone. But again, wait— Chris Snee is called for holding and the play comes back. Another penalty follows and the result is a disappointing field goal making the Cowboy lead, 24-20. On the next possession Romo and Owens strike again on a 50-yard scoring play.

By game's end, the season looks this way: six victories against teams whose records total 15-39, offset by losses against teams that are 16-2. Question is: Can the Giants beat a good team?

Cowboys receiver Patrick Crayton thinks the answer is no. "I think they tried to talk themselves into the game. I think when you are kind of scared of another team you have to talk yourself up to really give yourself a chance. I'm not going to say they were scared. We'll say they were worried."

Scared? Worried?

On the positive side, Shockey has had a career-high 12 catches for 129 yards and a touchdown. But he is seeing a half empty glass. "We have to finish what we start," he says. "It seems the opportunities are out there. We had some costly plays. Like I said, we have to finish what we started."

COWBOYS 31 • GIANTS 20 • (6-3)

So an opponent suggests that this team is scared. Some of the players and the coach are a bit testy about the result and the questions that follow. The media guys who follow the team are puzzling over what it means. Last season was different, but like this year, a 6-2 record turned to 6-3 and then the season disintegrated.

"A lot is riding on the Giants proving it can all turn out differently this time," writes Mike Vaccaro in *The New York Post*. "The perception of the franchise is 'just-close' contenders or fading pretenders. Right now, the Cowboys and Packers look like they belong on a different level, because they do.

A year ago, the Giants proved how easy it is to fall apart in seven weeks. This time, they can go another way."

The words from the team throughout the week all sound the same: "we're better than we were against the Cowboys."

November 18, 2007, in Detroit

Like the Giants, the Lions are 6-3, and at packed Ford Field, both teams' fans still hope their team will show they're for real.

The Giants encounter an interception-prone QB and a weak running game. But while the team piles up statistical highlight after statistical highlight—Strahan's three sacks, Manning's 28 completions for 283 yards without an interception, picks by Sam Madison, James Butler and Gibril Wilson—points are not part of the package. The Lions turn the ball over four times, three on interceptions. They gain 25 yards rushing and get only one first down on the ground. And yet the game is no romp for the Big Blue.

Gibril Wilson (26) grabbed one of three Giants interceptions against the Lions.

With every opportunity to win easily, the team spends much of the fourth quarter going "three and out" as Jacobs is sidelined with a hamstring injury. But they are protected by Butler's leaping pick in the end zone and Madison's 1:08 later.

Shaun O'Hara rushes to greet Madison after his last-minute interception. "I think I actually said, 'Thank you, Sam,' as I ran on the field," says O'Hara. "I personally thanked him for allowing us to get out of here with a win."

"We should have been able to run that clock out," guard Chris Snee added. "We didn't do our job."

The first major season-ending injury occurs when linebacker Mathias Kiwanuka breaks his left leg.

But the result—some might say "escape"—is all that counts.

"Once we got that last ball," Madison says, "It was a sigh of relief."

Sam Madison picked off Detroit QB Jon Kitna. Brandon Jacobs, opposite, had a combined 103 yards on offense including an 18-yard rush and a 34-yard pass reception.

GIANTS 16 • LIONS 10 • (7-3)

There's a positive feel in the week between the Lions and Vikings, as the Giants move through their NFC North portion of the schedule. The Giants may be missing their No. 1 back, but so are the Vikings, whose No. 1 is the record-setting rookie Adrian Peterson, sidelined with a knee injury. The Giants' Derrick Ward hopes to return but cannot. Reuben Droughns says he is ready to take on the No. 1 running back role; even

Running back **Chester Taylor**, stopped here by **Barry Cofield**, gained 77 yards, but it was three Minnesota touchdowns off of interceptions, opposite, that resulted in the worst loss of the season for the Giants.

rookie Ahmad Bradshaw, who hasn't rushed the ball yet in the regular season, says "It's a wonderful opportunity."

Some of the optimism is tempered by the memory of the stinging defeat by the Vikings in the teams' last meeting in 2005, also at Giants Stadium. That day the Vikings won, 24-21, on a late field goal after scoring touchdowns on a kickoff return, a punt return and an interception return, never before done in the NFL.

Coach makes sure no one forgets.

"They had little or no offense –130-some yards. And that's it. They had 12 rushing yards. And they beat us; they made a play on second-and-long with the score 21-21; they got the ball down and kicked a 48-yard field goal and beat us. Every man in that locker room was sick. So we did mention it."

November 25, 2007, in Giants Stadium vs. Minnesota

The unthinkable happens, and the doubts and doubters cannot be explained away. The Giants have their worst game of the season, even worse than the loss to the Vikings in 2005.

"I wish there was some simple explanation for this game, but there isn't," says Coughlin. "We played very, very poorly."

Once again, the Vikings get three touchdowns on returns, but today they are all on interceptions. Eli Manning is intercepted four times and Darren Sharper, Dwight Smith and Chad Greenway turn their picks into touchdowns. The fourth sets up another score in Minnesota's 41-17 victory. Now, the media has a target with a No. 10 in the center.

"Each Manning misfire," writes Paul Schwartz in *The New York Post*, "seemed to suck more air out of the rapidly-deflating Giants."

Michael Strahan says the way the Giants lost is "almost comical." But there is no laughing.

Droughns and Bradshaw give the Giants an adequate running game, but all other signs are negative.

"There is no excuse for today and there is no explanation for it," Coach says. "'I started the year off with 'talk is cheap, play the game,' and obviously there is not a lot to talk about here."

VIKINGS 41 • GIANTS 17 • (7-4)

Coach is certain that Eli will bounce back. Others, particularly the fans who call in to sports talk radio, are not so sure. Of course, Coach's opinion counts more than all others combined.

And Eli knows that sometimes a quarterback just has a bad day. "I talked to Peyton—he knows what it's like," Manning says of his

Whole Support
The Eli Questions

GIVEN HIS LAST NAME, the position he plays and the price the Giants paid to acquire his rights on draft day 2004, it seemed that Eli Manning would always face the most intense scrutiny. And that when he had a game such as the loss to the Vikings in which he threw four interceptions, three returned for touchdowns, the questions would be intensified.

But in 2007, there was a distinct response from Coach and teammates that surely made a difference as the season went on.

As Eli faced the media for more than 30 minutes the day after the Vikings loss, Michael Strahan was almost in awe of his fellow captain's stamina: "Damn, still grilling him, huh?" Strahan said.

Center Shaun O'Hara, another captain, said: "There's unsaid support, but if anybody felt we needed to say or do more, I'm sure there would be people crawling over each other to offer it. We're not talking about a four-year old kid, we're talking about a man."

The Vikings game resulted in media comments such as the following from Mike Freeman, a columnist on CBSSportsline.com: "Manning's head seems totally, royally, utterly discombobulated." And this from *New York Post* columnist Steve Serby: "His career had suddenly gone disturbingly backwards."

But through the noise, the voices of Manning's teammates and coaches made it clear they believed this difficult time would not last. "He has had some very, very good games here," said Coach Tom Coughlin. "Don't forget about that. He has the whole support of the locker room."

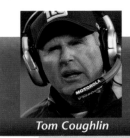

Tom Coughlin
A Sense of Team and Personal Reinvention

Tom Coughlin

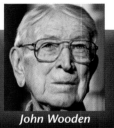

John Wooden

A CHARITY DINNER IN NEW JERSEY IN MAY 2007 had an impact that went beyond the cause it supported. It helped make the Giants' 2007 season a success.

That night, MAN (Minority Athletes Networking) Inc. presented its Man-of the-Year-award to Coach Tom Coughlin. The charity, founded by former Giants George Martin and Ron Johnson, also presented a lifetime achievement award to the 1986 Giants, winners of Super Bowl XXI.

While Coach Coughlin was clearly moved by the honor from the organization that is dedicated to making a difference in the lives of disadvantaged young people in the New York Metropolitan area, he was also struck by the togetherness of the '86 team, more than 20 years after the championship. "It's interesting to watch a group of very successful men gather together," Coughlin said. "To realize that as you move on in life, you have been on a team and you really understand and appreciate what a team is all about. The thing that they will always have is a common bond of camaraderie, which speaks so strongly for the true concept of 'team.'"

Harry Carson, the Giants'a Hall of Fame linebacker and a star of the '86 team, was the master of ceremonies that night. Carson, who still spends a lot of time around the Giants as co-host of a Giants pregame television show understood exactly what Coughlin was seeing and hearing. But he also saw big differences between the '86 team and others.

He said it's no secret why they remain so close: "Once you win, you are bonded. That is the way I feel about all of my teammates. And I think that is the way I think all of my teammates feel about me, or George Martin, or whoever. I think that connection is something that many of the players don't have now. And I think it is because of free agency—guys are about taking care of themselves and not about each other.

"I talk to some of the guys and I try to get them to understand what we went through playing ball," he said. "You are bonding with the guys who you run on the field with. It doesn't matter how old you get, where you go, what you do, you are still teammates. Just going back to those days when it was hot—we were all hot—and we all ran, and we all worked hard and we sacrificed."

Over the next few weeks, Coach Coughlin set up a Casino night for his current team and staff. By the time training camp started, the changes were evident.

"When somebody says they're going to change, you always wonder, 'Well, are they just saying that because it's training camp or it's the offseason?'" center Shaun O'Hara said to Jim Trotter of SI.com in October. "But when we were 0-2, Coach Coughlin didn't change. When we talk about putting egos aside, we're talking about a coach who has basically taken everything he's always done, and has said, 'OK, I'm going to change.' He almost reinvented himself.

"I think he's learned now that the players respond better to a coach who is a little bit more—I don't want to say soft—but who is interested and willing to take the time to get to know the players."

Coughlin was returning as a coach who had not won a playoff game in two tries with the Giants—a coach whose relationship with the media was often strained and who was perceived to have a stormy relationship with some players. During the offseason Coughlin, with the help of Giants VP of Communications Pat Hanlon, repaired some of his media relationships. He met individually with media who cover the team, for off-the-record straightforward talks.

"It was important for me to understand what they were feeling, and I did understand," he told SI.com's Trotter. "I don't always agree with them—and I certainly don't like the way I was treated at the end of the year—but they do have a job to do."

And over the course of the season, Coughlin made it known that he had also been influenced—for longer than just this year—by John Wooden, the great UCLA basketball coach.

The 97-year-old Wooden, who had never met Coughlin but had spoken with him on the phone, said to the Post's Mike Vaccaro: "Coach Coughlin's success on the field is a reflection of his principles, and I can think of no greater thing you can say about a coach."

For Coughlin, no words of wisdom from the great coach meant more than these: "You can make mistakes, but you are not a failure until you blame others for those mistakes. When you blame others you are trying to excuse yourself. When you make excuses you cannot properly evaluate yourself. Without proper evaluation, failure is inevitable."

brother who attended the Vikings game because his Colts played on Thanksgiving night. "He had a game a few weeks ago where he threw six interceptions. It just happens."

Then he reflects on the critical reaction to his "muted" postgame comments, and Easy Eli returns, wit intact: "The postgame press conference isn't the problem. It's what's happening on the field that needs to be corrected. I don't get to watch film of my postgame press conference."

The next day, the GM Jerry Reese is quoted as saying Manning looked "skittish" in the Vikings loss, and the storm continues.

"I wonder if Archie Manning is thinking 'My son, with his personality, can he handle New York?'" says Boomer Esiason, the former Jets quarterback and now a radio talker and someone who should know better. "Maybe he should be in Jacksonville. Maybe he should be in Atlanta or New Orleans."

You cannot think about the Giants' struggles and not think about what the absence of Brandon Jacobs means. Ward and Bradshaw fill in nicely, but Jacobs's presence is real and very important. When healthy, he gets the carries he is expected to get and gains the yards he is expected to gain and makes the impact he is expected to make.

Ahmad Bradshaw's longest gain was 11 yards as the Giants were held to 75 yards on the ground.

Then some terrible news shakes all of pro football, the death of the Redskins' Sean Taylor. Washington's 24-year-old safety was shot during a break-in at his home in Miami. Two Giants—Jeremy Shockey and Sinorice Moss—are former teammates of Taylor's at the University of Miami.

As the roiling week passes, the team's focus turns towards Chicago. The weather and the Bears await.

December 2, 2007, in Chicago

This is not an easy day, but why should it be? It's Chicago, it's December; there's fog and rain and, of course, wind. And the Bears are the defending NFC champions.

The Giants are still without Jacobs, but Derrick Ward carries the load and has a magical day with 154 yards rushing, a touchdown and two catches. But when he is tackled on a fourth-quarter run he feels "a pop" in his lower left leg. The leg is broken—virtually the same injury that now sidelines Mathias Kiwanuka.

The team is stifled by turnovers, three by Manning, another by Ward. But this is a different game from the Vikings game.

Late in the third quarter, Manning is driving the team toward the goal line and a chance to cut the Bears' nine-point lead. He has them at the one yard line and lobs a fade to Plaxico Burress. Intercepted.

The Bears first play after the interception gets them 44 yards and the dark evening gets darker. But the defense holds. And after an exchange of punts, the Giants have the ball again with 11:45 to play and 75 yards to go. Eleven plays later: touchdown Amani Toomer, a score made possible by a ruling from the replay booth. Ward's leg injury occurs on this drive, and Reuben Droughns replaces him.

It's 16-14 Bears, and the Giants' defense stops Rex Grossman again, helped by one of the team's six sacks. The Giants take over at their 23 with 4:55 to play. From above, Giants President John Mara, who has been staring out the back of the stadium at Lake Michigan, returns his focus to the field.

Droughns for 6; Manning to David Tyree (his first catch of the season) for 8; Droughns fumbles the next carry when hit but he recovers and the gain is 3; Manning to Toomer for 15 and another first down.

From his first victory as the Giants' quarterback against Dallas in 2004, it has

Jeremy Shockey, above, landed awkwardly after this catch, but held on to the ball. Chicago quarterback **Rex Grossman**, opposite, was sacked six times by the swarming defense of the Giants. **Derrick Ward**, below, having already racked up huge yardage, broke his leg in the fourth quarter.

become clear that Eli Manning is made for late-game drives. The spirit so many think is lacking is apparent and his grace under pressure is unquestioned. This is Eli time.

Droughns off left guard for four; Manning to Tyree for 24. Two minutes to play. Droughns for no gain and then Manning to Burress for 15, a play upheld by replay. First down at the 2.

Droughns around right end for two yards and the touchdown.

Speaking of Manning later, linebacker Antonio Pierce tells John Branch of the *Times*, "I don't know what that guy's built of or what he's got inside of him. But I tell you what—for all the heat he takes and everything that's been going on the last couple weeks, I don't know if

The *Benefits of Health*
Working Around Injuries

Mathias Kiwanuka shifted from defensive end to linebacker in 2007, but broke his left leg against the Lions, ending his season after just ten games.

"WE LOST TO PHILADELPHIA IN THE PLAYOFFS on a last-play field goal," GM Jerry Reese said about the 2006 season. "We were missing two of our best defensive ends, one of our top two wide receivers, our starting left tackle and a starting linebacker. And we only lost by three points."

So, no, Reese said, he wasn't surprised that a healthy Giants team could make a strong run in 2007.

Injuries are such a significant part of a pro football season, but you can't plan for when they will happen or to whom. All you can do is have a well-conditioned team and a strong set of backups, and hope for the best

In 2007, despite devastating injuries to Mathias Kiwanuka, a starting linebacker, Derrick Ward, an important running back, and Jeremy Shockey, the starting tight end, the Giants escaped the worst of what might have been.

Perhaps the best example of those "escaped" possibilities came following week one, when Eli Manning and Osi Umenyiora were each expected to miss a game or two—Eli with an injured shoulder, Osi with an injured knee. But for game two, both Eli and Osi were out there—no games missed.

If injuries to one player more than others tended to "nag" the team this season, they were those to running back Brandon Jacobs who, in total, missed the better part of six games. But Ward ran effectively as his replacement until he broke his leg. And soon after, Jacobs was able to return.

Meanwhile, the offensive line was the only one in the NFL to play the entire regular season as a unit. Throughout the lineup, severe injuries did not come all at once, giving time for replacements to fit in.

anybody else could handle the pressure and do what he did."

The Giants have the lead, but they may have left too much time. The Bears' dangerous return man Devin Hester takes the kickoff back to the Chicago 41. On first down, Grossman connects with Adrian Peterson on a short pass with a lot of open field. But the Giants' Michael Johnson makes a shoestring tackle and limits him to a two-yard gain. However, Grossman is not done. The Bears get one first down, then (on fourth and 15) another. There are 17 seconds to play and 28 yards to go. First down incomplete; second down incomplete. Third down is broken up by James Butler at the goal line and the game ends.

"It wasn't the prettiest," Manning says. "At times, it was flat-out ugly. But it was sweet."

Every yard was a struggle for both teams in a game that went down to the final play.

GIANTS 21 • BEARS 16 • (8-4)

A tough part of the schedule is over—Big Blue vs. the NFC's black and blue division, the North. And the results reflect the Giants' season: two losses at home, two wins on the road. The losses are ugly, almost deflating. The victories come by a total of 11 points.

"When we are on the road it is a very tight environment," says Coughlin. "It's our team. We are together all of the time. We go right from the practice field to the shower to the bus to the airport. The feeling of being together is very strong on the road. Nobody there cares about you except the guys that you are with."

Injuries could take a toll—Kiwanuka and Ward are lost for the season; Jacobs is hobbling and uncertain of his return. Burress's ankle keeps him from practice, and Antonio Pierce, Aaron Ross, James Butler and Gibril Wilson are all hurting. But Burress and Pierce keep playing, and the rookie replacements are filling in convincingly for injured starters.

During the week, Strahan has a conversation with the *Times*' John Branch and says if the Giants win the Super Bowl, "we'd have to call it a day." And then he laughs.

Ahead, the Eagles. The good news: it's on the road.

December 9, 2007, in Philadelphia

Brandon Jacobs, opposite, returned from injury and bulled his way for 70 yards against the Eagles. **Barry Cofield**, below, was credited with two tackles and one sack.

The Giants may have won five of six road games already but few were pretty. The seventh road game is no different. The starting safeties James Butler and Gibril Wilson are out, and their replacements are the rookies Michael Johnson and Craig Dahl, the latter a free agent from North Dakota State making his first start. Pierce plays despite a sprained ankle and no practice. Jacobs returns but shows the effect of his interrupted season, gaining 70 yards but losing two fumbles. Again, the offense scores only one touchdown.

"It was an incredible game," Coach says when it's over. Fourteen weeks into the season and the optimism is still showing.

"Our two rookie safeties did an outstanding job," Coughlin says. "When you put Aaron Ross in the nickel package, we had three rookies in the secondary against Donovan McNabb. That was quite an accomplishment by those young guys."

Manning has 17 completions for 219 yards and the one touchdown. But most important, he has no interceptions. This is the defense's day. After giving up a touchdown on the first Eagles' possession, the defense allowed only two David Akers field goals. It had three more sacks and again gave McNabb fits. The Eagles fans treat the Giants with their usual contempt.

"We have a road warrior mentality," says defensive end Justin Tuck. "We thrive on the boos; we thrive on the fans saying we stink."

When David Akers' 57-yard field goal attempt plunks off the upright as time runs out, the Giants have what they came for. Unsightly or incredible, a win is a win.

GIANTS 16 • EAGLES 13 • (9-4)

Those asking the questions want to talk about the playoffs. The players know what they need to do to guarantee a spot. So do the coaches. But you won't catch them talking about it.

"We don't have anything secured," says Coughlin, "and we are playing as hard as we can to get to where we know that we are playing our best football. And that certainly is not the case just yet. We have the Washington Redskins, a team that came off a big win last week, and we have got to get ourselves ready."

December 16, 2007, in Giants Stadium vs. Washington

A lot of things happen in and around this game, none of them good. The night before: tragedy. As always on the evening before a home game, the players and coaches gather in a hotel for meetings and meals and a chance to have a quieter night's sleep. While the team is in meetings, David Tyree's wife comes to the hotel with terrible news for her husband: His mother Thelma has died suddenly in Florida after suffering a heart attack. Tyree leaves to be with his family.

On Sunday morning, the Giants' practice bubble deflates in a New York area winter storm.

The game is devastating. After Jacobs runs for 17 on the Giants' second play of the game, Manning throws three straight incomplete passes in the wind, and the Giants punt. That sets the tone as Eli is 18 of 53—his 35 incompletes being the most by an NFL quarterback in 40 years. Jacobs runs for 130 yards on 25 carries but also drops five passes. The team drops 12 of Eli's passes.

On the other side of the ball, the Giants are facing Todd Collins, a quarterback who has not started a game in 10 years. But Collins was the NFC Offensive Player of the Week after replacing an injured Jason Campbell in a Skins victory over the Bears the previous Thursday night. Collins is adequate tonight, completing only eight passes but he protects the ball and his team.

Fred Robbins, opposite, finished with four tackles and this sack of Redskins QB **Todd Collins**. **Eli Manning**, below, has a tough day as do his receivers who drop 12 passes in windy conditions.

For the Giants, the missed passes are not the only catastrophe. In the third quarter Jeremy Shockey is blocking on a Jacobs run when he and Amani Toomer get entangled. Shockey's injury is the third broken left fibula suffered by Giants players in five games (Ward and Kiwanuka also have the fracture). But this one seems to disrupt the team immediately.

At the end, given the dismal passing and receiving, fans and media are left to wonder why the Giants did not run the ball more. There is no immediate answer.

"They wanted it more than us tonight," says co-captain Antonio Pierce. "You could tell by the way they played."

Coughlin is asked about the play selection and says: "I think we

New Men in Town
The Rookie Contribution

Jay Alford was one of many Giants rookies who contributed to the team's success.

CHAMPIONSHIP TEAMS DON'T WIN WITH ROOKIES playing major roles. It's a rule. The sky is blue, water is wet, and savvy vets win titles. Sure a first- or second-round choice might see time on the field, but later picks are usually headed for special teams at best, or become practice-squad fodder.

The 2007 New York Giants broke all the rules. All eight draft picks made the roster; seven played key roles; six started at different times during the season. Even Michael Matthews, an undrafted rookie free agent, was a major force as the team's blocking tight end. When safeties Gibril Wilson and James Butler went down with injuries it was Craig Dahl, another undrafted free agent, who teamed with seventh-round pick Michael Johnson (224th overall) when Big Blue marched into Philadelphia.

Ahmad Bradshaw (No. 250 overall) started the season as a shaky return man but by year's end had teamed with Brandon Jacobs to provide the "Thunder and Lightning" combination in the Giants' backfield.

Quiet Kevin Boss had a vastly different personality than brash Jeremy Shockey, but when the All-Pro suffered a broken leg, Boss—the 153rd player selected—showed that his hands were just as soft.

On the special teams, Zak DeOssie (116th overall) and third-round pick Jay Alford (81st) gave straight and true snaps to the kicking game—DeOssie the long snapper for punts, Alford for field goals and extra points. "I never saw any team have two rookies play that role," said placekicker Lawrence Tynes. "I always had my own snapper and that's all he did. But these guys were great."

Of course, the top two picks played key roles as well. First-rounder Aaron Ross and second-rounder Steve Smith fought through injuries to make key contributions both in the regular season and, especially, in the playoffs.

always intended to mix. My thought was that if we went into the no-huddle mode we might get something going."

That never happens. The many passes extend the game almost to midnight, and few fans remain at the end. Those who do feel as deflated as that practice bubble.

"Forget about the playoffs," right tackle Kareem McKenzie says. "Right now it's about playing better football. No way, shape or form we should be performing like this."

REDSKINS 22 • GIANTS 10 • (9-5)

The Giants are left with the real possibility that they may have to forget about the playoffs. Ahead are games on the road with 7-7 Buffalo and at home with the unbeaten Patriots. The weather is sure to be brutal in Buffalo, and the Patriots will be fired up, hoping to complete a 16-0 season.

After the Redskins game, Mike Vaccaro of the *Post* declares the season over: The Giants were assaulted with the harsh and stinging reality that whatever pretense they had at making serious January noise had ended on this frigid night in East Rutherford. Next year arrived 16 days early in New Jersey."

The wind played havoc with **Jeff Feagles'** punting game in Giants Stadium.

ACT THREE
SAFE HARBOR

The Giants ground attack combined for almost 300 yards against the Bills. **Ahmad Bradshaw** gained 151 yards including an 88-yard TD and **Brandon Jacobs**, above, gained 143 more, scoring twice.

THE SEASON IS NOT OVER. The Giants have two games left and are in an excellent position for the playoffs. They have the best record of four teams in the running for the NFC's two wildcard slots. The tiebreaking scenarios all favor the other teams, but there's no tiebreaking if your team has the best record. A win and they're in.

There is a sense of desperation among fans as the team gets ready to go off to Buffalo. The players, benefiting from a season of relative good health and complete comfort in the locker room, seem to relish it.

"This is the best place for this team," says Antonio Pierce. "Backs against the wall, hearing the whole hoopla about how we're desperate and need to win. We love it."

Times columnist William Rhoden makes an odd projection: "Unfortunately, it involves the Giants losing to Buffalo. And New England extends its record to 15-0 by crushing Miami. That sets up a monumental season finale at Giants Stadium… I would be curious to see, once and for all, what is in Manning's tank."

The players and coaches know what's in Eli's tank.

December 23, 2007, in Buffalo

With everything needing to go right, in the opening minutes nothing does. Buffalo's rookie quarterback Trent Edwards takes the field as if he's the one who needs to prove something quickly. Seven plays, a touchdown pass, and the Bills lead, 7-0. It's cold, it's raining, the winds are gusting; and this is as good as the weather is going to be.

On their second possession the Bills score on another Edwards pass.

This is not going as planned.

The Bills, already eliminated from playoff contention, seem buoyed by the presence of Kevin Everett, their tight end, grievously injured in the season opener against Denver. Everett appears to have overcome the paralysis that struck that day following his tackle of the Broncos' kick returner Domenik Hixon, who is now running back kicks for the Giants.

As the weather worsens, the Giants gain some traction. After a Buffalo fumble in the second quarter, the Giants take five plays to go 23 yards to score on a touchdown by Brandon Jacobs. Ominously, the drive is almost short-circuited by a Manning fumble, quickly recovered (the second such notation to appear on the score sheet and not the last).

Ahmad Bradshaw
Arrives and Answers

Bradshaw displays his scuffed helmet after his 88-yard touchdown run against the Bills.

IN TRAINING CAMP FOR THE 2007 SEASON, one of the most overlooked position battles was between Ryan Grant and Ahmad Bradshaw for the last running back spot. Bradshaw had a lot to overcome, including the perceived stigma of being the Giants' last draft pick and a past that included two minor incidents with the law as a teenager in Virginia. But On September 1, Bradshaw won the competition, and Grant was shipped to the Green Bay Packers, where he became their leading rusher.

After the first two weeks of the season, you would have had to forgive Giants fans (and perhaps some members of the team) who wondered if the organization had made the wrong decision. Bradshaw opened the season returning kicks, and in his first two games did not distinguish himself, fumbling twice.

Bradshaw played sparingly for much of the remainder of the season, having toted the ball only six times for 39 yards going into Week 16 against the Bills. Still, there was a lot about Bradshaw that was intriguing. An ankle injury to Brandon Jacobs in Buffalo gave the young running back his first big chance, and this time he did not disappoint anyone, rushing for 151 yards—the highest total by a Giants rookie in 57 years—including an 88-yard touchdown.

"He reminds me a little bit of Tiki [Barber]," said offensive coordinator Kevin Gilbride. "I don't know that Tiki moved the pile the way he does, but the quickness resembles him—the ability to change direction, his vision, which those great runners have."

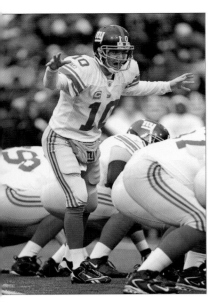

With his ground game working, **Eli** attempted only 11 pases against the Bills.

Soon, things turn the Giants' way. Jeff Feagles is run into on a fourth-down punt, and the penalty changes a Bills first down at their 19 into a Giants first down at the Bills 43. On the next play, Jacobs shows his inner John Riggins and goes 43 yards for a touchdown, his longest run as a pro.

The deficit is gone. And when Lawrence Tynes kicks a bad-weather-defying field goal late in the second quarter, somehow the Giants are leading by 3 at the half.

But Eli's first pass of the second half is intercepted. The Bills' rookie running back Marshawn Lynch quickly scores and the Giants' lead is gone. Meanwhile, the Giants decide to stop attempting the impossible and put the brakes on their passing game.

On the next drive they have 14 plays, 12 of them runs. But they get nothing when Reuben Droughns is stopped on fourth down at the Bills' goal line.

Next is another Eli fumble, this one lost to Buffalo at the Bills' 12.

In the Giants defensive huddle, Kawika Mitchell has a vision: "He pointed to the right part of the end zone and said he was going to get a tipped ball and run it in," says Antonio Pierce. "We joked and laughed, but then he did it."

That puts the Giants back in the lead. The rain changes to snow as the temperature drops. The Giants' defense is strong now, averting danger following Eli's second intercepted pass.

After a Bills punt pins the Giants deep, rookie running back Ahmad Bradshaw, replacing Jacobs, has a vision of his own, which Manning shares postgame: "He said, 'I'm gonna take it to the house and end this game.'"

And so he does. He goes 88 yards for a score and the third-longest

FAN•POST

I don't live far from Rich Stadium in Buffalo and I usually go to one Bills game a year courtesy of a buddy with a ticket connection. The Giants were coming and I was extra excited when I saw the date, December 23...my 41st birthday.

I told my buddy to dress warm and be ready for rain. He showed up in a sweatshirt and jean jacket. No rain gear, nothing warm.

By the time we got to our seats, it was 14-0 Buffalo and it had started to rain. My buddy and I figured as long as the rain was not blowing in our faces, we would be OK. Wrong. I had insulated ski pants and rain gear so I was fine but my buddy was not. Before half time he had enough. I was afraid he would want me to leave, too, and miss my birthday game. But he handed me $20, said happy birthday and went to the car. I made friends with the Giants' fans around me and had a few adult beverages.

By the time the Giants won, my buddy had been sitting in the car for almost two hours. We've been friends for over 20 years but I can't believe what he put up with so I could enjoy my birthday. He even tolerated my happy inebriated state on the drive home.

Steve Levine
Rochester, NY

touchdown run in Giants history. As he explodes through the line, following his blocks, the snow seems to burst loose, as if fans throwing confetti are hailing the young back.

When Corey Webster intercepts an Edwards pass and returns it for a touchdown, the victory is assured. The Giants are in the playoffs for the third straight season, as good a streak as the franchise has ever had.

GIANTS 38 • BILLS 21 • (10-5)

Everyone feels good.

Coughlin gets a laugh when he tells of his celebratory dousing as the game ends. "It was the chunks of ice that gave me some mixed thoughts about exactly what the intention was there," Coughlin says.

Amani Toomer remembers when the Giants were not such happy campers. "There have been years here where the offense didn't like the defense and everybody was mad at the special teams," he says. "When Coach Coughlin came here, it calmed all that down."

Now the attention turns to New England, coming to Giants Stadium on Saturday night, hoping to complete the first 16-0 season in NFL history. There's so much interest, the NFL announces that this game, originally scheduled for the NFL Network, will also be seen in prime time on partner networks CBS and NBC. In New York, with the proper cable options, fans will be able to watch the game on four outlets. The last time the NFL had a simulcast similar to this was Super Bowl I, when CBS and NBC both did the game—but that time with different broadcasters in the booth.

It is clear what New England will do: play its starters and play to win. What is not so clear is what the Giants will do. Their playoff position is assured, their first round opponent determined. Many say rest the starters, avoid injury.

Two key Giants who have been troubled by injuries all season want nothing to do with that. "No one in here is screaming 'Let's rest,' I can tell you that," Brandon Jacobs says.

After practicing for just the third time all season, Plaxico Burress says: "I don't think it's a benefit for us to

With both teams playing their strongest lineup, New England's **Stephen Gostkowski** tees up the ball for the opening kickoff of the last game of the regular season. The Patriots are looking to "run the table" and go into the playoffs undefeated.

Michael Strahan takes the field for what may be his last home game after 15 seasons as a Giant.

take (a week) off," he says. "When you get into the playoffs, it's a different speed – the game is faster. Decisions have to be made quicker and that's the mode that we're trying to get ourselves into."

The team's playoff opponent, the Tampa Bay Buccaneers, make their intentions clear in game 15 when they pull their starters late in a loss. They say they'll rest many of them in their upcoming game as well.

The media weighs in. *Times* columnist Harvey Araton tells Coughlin to play for the upset. On his blog at NYPost.com, beat writer Paul Schwartz says: Start everyone, play to win, have a plan to get the regulars out. And let Eli end his night on a high note. *Post* columnist Steve Serby is the most direct: "Play to win the damn game."

From New England, advice comes from an unusual source: "I think definitely Strahan and Osi should take the weekend off. I'd rest them. I'll be lobbying for that. Coach Coughlin, if you're listening, definitely rest those guys."

The lobbyist? New England's quarterback Tom Brady.

After keeping his thoughts private for several days—claiming to have consulted everyone including the janitor—Coughlin reveals his decision. "Our objective is to win," he says. "That's what we work for, that's what we prepare for, that's what we practice for. And it will be no different this week."

No one who follows the Giants and pays attention to Coughlin and his players—what they say, how they act—is surprised.

December 29, 2007, in Giants Stadium vs. New England

The stands are full, of course, but more than a few in the crowd are rooting for the Patriots. Missing for New York is the rookie clairvoyant Ahmad Bradshaw, sidelined with a bruised calf. But all the Giants' starters are on the field. Watching on TV are almost 35 million viewers, the largest audience for a non-playoff game in 12 years.

The players on both teams give one of the most memorable regular season performances in NFL history. Eli Manning completes 22 of 32 for 251 yards and four touchdowns. The Giants' new man Domenik Hixon runs back a kickoff for a touchdown. The team gets an efficient running game from Brandon Jacobs. They get two aerial touchdowns—from Plaxico Burress and Jeremy Shockey's rookie replacement Kevin Boss.

Early in the third quarter, the Giants are leading by 12 when the Patriots come back. A 65-yard pass play from Brady to Randy Moss gives the Patriots a lead and gives Brady the record for most touchdown passes in a season (50), breaking the record of Eli's older brother Peyton. For Moss, in a season of career resurrection, it is touchdown No. 23, breaking the record of the great Jerry Rice.

When the Patriots follow Eli's only interception of the night with another touchdown, it seems the Giants have fought the good fight and lost.

But they are not done. Using the no-huddle offense that seems to give him confidence, Eli guides the team 68 yards in 11 plays, and the Patriots' lead is cut to 3 with 64 seconds to play.

When Lawrence Tynes's onside kick is covered by the Pats' Steve Vrabel, this remarkable game ends. The Patriots get their unbeaten regular season and the Giants get respect.

"There's nothing but positives," Coughlin says. "I don't have any negatives about this game. We had everything to gain and nothing to lose."

PATRIOTS 38 • GIANTS 35 • (10-6)

The Giants were able to pressure quarterback **Tom Brady**. **Justin Tuck**, above, and **Reggie Torbor**, below, both work to deny him time and space.

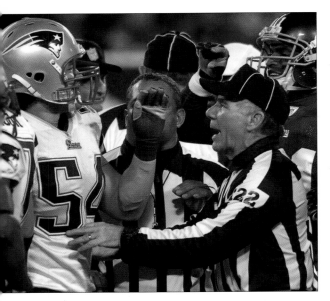

Tedy Bruschi and **Amani Toomer** disagree.

While some of the fears about playing the game full-tilt are realized—linebacker Kawika Mitchell and center Shaun O'Hara each sprains a knee and cornerback Sam Madison strains an abdominal muscle—there is no denying that the Giants get what they played for.

Steve Serby from the *Post* writes: "Coughlin would have chased Bill Belichick and Tom Brady out into the parking lot if they'd let him. And his Giants would have followed him."

Captain Antonio Pierce says: "We attacked that quarterback. We hit him."

The final approval comes from team President John Mara. "They feel that if they played that well against the best team in the league, they have a chance against anybody."

Without Practice
Plaxico Burress

PLAXICO BURRESS HAD ONE STRANGE 2007 SEASON. The lanky, mercurial wide receiver fought through knee and ankle pain, and while his teammates practiced and reporters scurried to find out his status; Burress worked with trainers and doctors and acupuncturists and studied his playbook to make sure that as each game rolled around, No. 17 would be on the field.

"I've always said I think we need him out there to practice," Eli Manning said after Burress racked up 97 yards on six catches against Atlanta. "Now I'm starting to maybe think we don't. I don't know why it's working, but he's making some big plays for us."

Burress always managed to get on the field for the games and led the team in all receiving categories. Plaxico's practice of not practicing amazed his teammates.

"He's going to be the first guy to play all 16 games and not practice," Antonio Pierce said, calling Burress his new role model.

For Burress, the faith Coach Tom Coughlin had in him was vital. "He had enough trust in me that I could go out and be successful when I was 70 or 75 percent."

But Coach got contemplative after Burress helped knock off the Eagles in December for a second time with seven catches for 136 yards and a touchdown: "It makes you wonder what Plax and Eli could do if they were ever able to practice together."

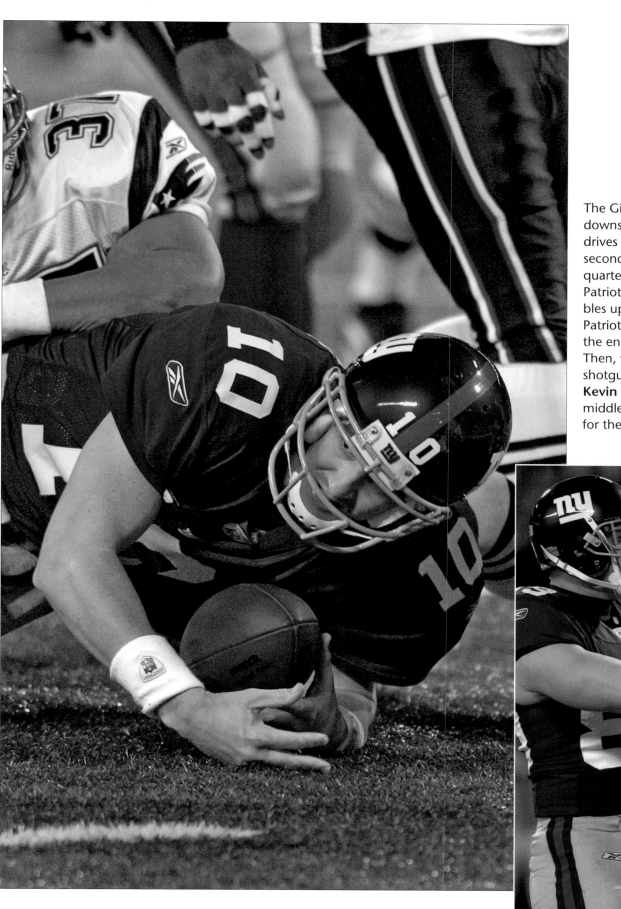

The Giants score touchdowns at the end of long drives late in both the second and fourth quarters against the Patriots. **Eli**, left, scrambles up the middle to the Patriots three yard line at the end of the first half. Then, working from the shotgun he connects with **Kevin Boss**, below, in the middle of the end zone for the score.

ACT FOUR
FACING THE SIRENS

Jeff Garcia had a history of playing well against the Giants in the playoffs. **Amani Toomer**, opposite, caught seven passes including this fourth-quarter touchdown.

TOM COUGHLIN HAS NOT WON a playoff game as the Giants coach; Eli Manning has not won one as quarterback; the team has not won a playoff game since beating Minnesota in the NFC championship on January 14, 2001. If these facts don't change on Sunday, there will surely be major alterations coming.

Some wonder if the team is too satisfied at having played well against the Patriots.

"I told the team that this would be a positive experience for us," Coughlin says, "and we would gain momentum from the game, and we did... We didn't win. We all know that."

Buccaneers Coach Jon Gruden has rested his starters for most of their last two games. Jeff Garcia has sat for the last game and a half, and over the past five games has thrown only 45 passes. However, his greatest days in the NFL have come against the Giants—in the 2002 playoffs for the 49ers and last season for the Eagles.

Heading into the playoffs Garcia, it seems, prefers a different approach. "I feel over-rested," he says.

Gruden rejects any criticism. "Momentum is having your quarterback healthy and walking around feeling good," he says.

The Giants get a lift from the outspoken Ronde Barber, Tiki's twin and a cornerback for the Buccaneers. He offers opinions on Eli Manning, ("he can be had, we know that") and Plaxico Burress ("not overly fast" or "athletic"). Burress prints out the quotes and posts them above his locker.

Reality hits before the game Sunday, when the Giants announce their inactive players—Sam Madison and Shaun O'Hara are out. O'Hara's absence is the first for an offensive lineman this season. Kawika Mitchell will not start. O'Hara's replacement is Grey Ruegamer, Mitchell's starting spot is taken by Gerris Wilkinson, and Madison is replaced by Corey Webster, who has been something of a disappointment to the Giants.

On signs held by fans:

TURN #27 THE BEAST LOOSE!

JFK to Tampa $1232.50
night @ the Marriot
Tix to the game $
NFL playoffs on
...PRICELE...

ny SuperBowl Combos:
1987- Simms to Bavaro
1991- Hostetler to Baker
2008-Manning to Burress
AZ Bound !

Ronde
Loose Lips
Sink Ships
Big Blue

Ahmad Bradshaw savors his first NFL postseason victory. He finished with 66 yards rushing.

January 6, 2008 • NFC Wild Card Playoff in Tampa

As expected, the weather is warm, and many Giants fans find their way to Raymond James Stadium. What is not expected is how efficiently Eli Manning plays. He completes 20 of 27 with no interceptions and two touchdowns. His passes do not go long, but they go to the right people.

"I missed a few short ones early," he says. "My thought process was to play really safe, don't force anything. You want to get the ball out quick; don't throw interceptions, and don't stay back there too long where they can cause a fumble."

Brandon Jacobs and Ahmad Bradshaw combine for 100 yards rushing, and Jacobs scores two touchdowns, one running and one receiving; Amani Toomer catches Eli's other scoring pass. Toomer's touchdown caps the most significant offensive series of the day, a 92-yard drive that uses up more than eight minutes. His touchdown completes a 24-0 run for the Giants.

The team so plagued by turnovers all season suffers none. And they seize three key Buccaneer turnovers. First, Webster recovers a fumble on the opening kickoff of the second half, leading to a Lawrence Tynes field goal. Then he stops a Bucs drive by intercepting a Garcia pass at the goal line. Webster is finding his way back into his coach's good graces. With two minutes to go, R.W. McQuarters stops the Bucs last good scoring chance with another interception.

When the Giants leave the field, their fans serenade them.

Coach has his first playoff victory, as does Eli, and the team has ended its playoff losing streak.

GIANTS 24 • BUCCANEERS 14 • (11-6)

Re-defining
Corey Webster

ONE OF THE *WEBSTER'S DICTIONARY* DEFINITIONS of roller coaster is, "a period of prosperity, happiness, security, or the like, followed by a contrasting period of ... depression, despair, or the like."

Turn that around and it might equally apply to the 2007 season of Corey Webster.

Coming into the league in 2005, Webster had a reputation as a ball hawk and solid tackler (in three seasons at LSU he recorded 115 tackles and 16 interceptions). But entering his third NFL season in 2007 Webster had yet to live up to that reputation. Both his role and his prospects diminished as the season progressed. Kevin Dockery and first-round draft pick Aaron Ross were given more playing time while Webster was relegated to special teams, and eventually the bench.

As the season wore on, injuries to others gave Webster another chance. In the playoff-clinching game against the Bills, he sealed the win for the Giants by returning an interception 34 yards for a touchdown.

Webster said the difference this season was the style brought to the defense by Coordinator Steve Spagnuolo: "He's very aggressive. We go out and make plays happen."

Against Tampa in the Wild-Card game, he had an interception and a fumble recovery. He also held the dangerous Joey Galloway to one nine-yard catch. Against Green Bay he stopped Brett Favre with an interception in overtime.

It took a while for Webster to find his place again, but he used the playoffs to prove that he had.

The reward is another trip to Texas Stadium to face the Division champion Cowboys.

"It's not going to be easy; we've got a tough challenge against Dallas; we played them twice this year," says Manning. "But, I think third time could be a charm."

Easy E? Predicting a win? A reporter asks, "Does that mean you're guaranteeing a victory?"

Manning smiles and says, "No more stupid questions, please."

And everyone laughs.

In Dallas's first season in the league in 1960, the only game they avoided losing was a tie with the Giants. Having a coach, Tom Landry, who had spent most of his career as a player and coach with the Giants, the Cowboys became natural rivals for Big Blue. After 91 games against one another, this is their first meeting in the playoffs. With their victory on opening night, the Cowboys quickly reversed all the Giants' optimism. When the teams played again after the Giants had won six in a row, the Cowboys did it again. As Eli notes, the Giants are getting a third chance.

Dallas quarterback **Tony Romo**'s pregame trip to Mexico with Jessica Simpson became fodder for call-in shows and in-stadium heckling.

In the spirit of a nation obsessed with celebrity, all eyes are on the remarkably celebrated Dallas quarterback Tony Romo.

Romo's social life has become as well covered as his life in football. While the Giants are preparing for Tampa Bay, the Cowboy quarterback is photographed in Cabo San Lucas, Mexico, with his girlfriend, singer-actress Jessica Simpson, her parents and Romo's teammate Jason Witten. When he returns, the questions are about the trip and not his expectations for the game. The Giants are more intrigued by Romo's last three games—five interceptions, one touchdown pass and two Cowboy losses.

Cowboys receiver Terrell Owens tells fans to "get your popcorn ready" to watch his performance.

The Giants seem the more focused team—a result, among other factors, of having had to win their way into the playoffs, face down the Patriots and defeat the Buccaneers. It's a good time of year to concentrate on football.

January 13, 2008 • NFC Divisional Playoff in Dallas

The sign outside the visitors' locker room jibes Owens. "Getcha Popcorn Ready" it says. The Romo storm goes on all week. For the Giants, another earlier piece of news is surely more important. The Cowboys will send 12 players to the Pro Bowl; the Giants will send one, Osi Umenyiora.

"It's like an all-Pro team versus an all-Joe team," Giants linebacker Antonio Pierce says. But he's smart enough to know that the most important upcoming trips are to Green Bay and Glendale, Arizona, not to Hawaii.

Patrick Crayton's comments from November (the Giants, he said, were "kinda scared") are repeated this week, and the New Yorkers take note.

The biggest worry for the Giants is in their defensive secondary—Sam Madison and Kevin Dockery are still out. What is not yet known, of course, is that Aaron Ross will dislocate his shoulder in the third quarter, to be replaced by Geoffrey Pope who hadn't played in a game all season.

As the game unfolds, pregame focus shows—in the end, the Giants have three penalties for 25 yards, the Cowboys 11 for 84. The Giants again do not turn over the ball; the Cowboys do so only once, but it's at the right time in the right place for the Giants.

What the Cowboys do well today is control the football, using more than ten minutes of the second quarter to go 90 yards in 20 plays to take the lead.

"I have never been that tired before," says Antonio Pierce.

The Giants get the ball with 53 seconds left in the half at their 29. Eli takes them on a perfect series, using only 46 seconds and one timeout. The final play is a four-yard touchdown pass to Amani Toomer, and the teams are tied.

This 25-yard punt return by **R.W. McQuarters**, opposite, started a 37-yard scoring drive that put the Giants in the lead early in the fourth quarter. **Tony Romo**, below, bested Eli in most offensive categories except on the scoreboard.

Another long Cowboy drive starts the second half but ends with just a field goal. Then late in the third quarter Manning does it again, following a 25-yard punt return by R.W. McQuarters. He passes to Toomer and twice to Steve Smith. Ahmad Bradshaw runs for eight yards around the end to the 1. Then, doing what he does best, Jacobs powers it in from a yard out for the touch-down. The Giants have the lead.

Four punts, two by each team follow, and the Cowboys take over on the Giants 48 with plenty of time to score. Romo seems ready to silence the critics. He completes three passes and gets two runs from Marion Barber for a first down on the Giants 22 with 31 seconds to play. A Cowboy penalty is followed by a short completion to Witten, then an incomplete to Witten and another to Patrick Crayton.

The target on fourth down is Terry Glenn. But the pass is picked off by McQuarters.

"Terry ran a little skinny post," says McQuarters. "I knew they had to take a shot, it was fourth down. Gibril Wilson was in a good position, I was in a good position, and I was able to get my head around and get my hands up in time… I was thinking catch it, catch it, get down, end the game, let's go home."

And he does.

The Cowboys streak of failing to win a playoff game extends to 11 seasons. The Giants season extends north.

GIANTS 21 • COWBOYS 17 • (12-6)

ny FAN•POST

My daughter was born after the week two loss to Green Bay.

It was a low time as the team had dropped to 0-2 on the season. Their next game was at Washington and the Giants turned the season around with a tremendous goal line stand. I remember thinking my daughter might be a good luck charm. Sure enough, the Giants went on a six-game winning streak.

While the season had its ups and downs, something felt different to me. Maybe it was the influx of new talent from what may be one of the most talented rookie classes the Giants have ever seen. Maybe it was that I was now able to watch Giants games with my own baby girl.

The playoff run was remarkable. Beating Dallas in Dallas was one of the greatest feelings I've ever had as a Giants fan. My great memory is the picture we took as the clock went to :00. It's me with my daughter sitting next to the television with the disgusted face of Cowboy owner Jerry Jones on the screen.

Brennan Neill
Burlington, VT

Brandon Jacobs, opposite, pounds in what would prove to be the game-winning touchdown. **R.W. McQuarters**, below, snuffed out Dallas's last drive with an interception in the end zone

Wide receiver **David Tyree** after defeating Dallas; much accomplished but there's a long road still to be traveled.

The mood has changed just about everywhere except among the Giants themselves. Fans who doubted are believers. The media that follow the Giants, including those who have come along lately, all seem to be rooting if not for the team then surely for the story. Everyone has hitched up a wagon. Everyone that is but Packers fans and New Englanders. The TV audience for the Cowboys game is 40.1 million. The country is paying attention.

Meanwhile, Green Bay has eliminated Seattle and the focus has turned naturally to quarterback Brett Favre and the weather. It's going to be cold in Green Bay.

Small adjustments are made: Eli Manning will play with a glove on his non-throwing hand; extra undergarments will surely be worn; heaters will line the sidelines. The most telling comment of the week comes from the Giants only native of Wisconsin, guard Rich Seubert whose hometown of Rozellville is a football reference in its own right.

"Long as it's not 78 on their side and zero on our side, who really cares about the weather?" Seubert says to the *Times*' Harvey Araton.

Coughlin names honorary captains—Hall-of-Fame Giants linebacker Harry Carson and Lt. Col. Greg Gadson whose visit to the team back in Washington in Week 3 helped inspire their first win.

The best news for the Giants is that Aaron Ross has returned to practice and Coach expects him to play.

Coughlin is asked by a huge media contingent during the week if he's enjoying this. He says, "Every second. Can't you tell?" Then he breaks into a broad smile.

January 20, 2008 • NFC Championship in Green Bay

The weather is worse than expected. The temperature is the third coldest ever recorded for an NFL game—minus-1 with a wind chill of minus-23. The cold makes it a little harder to pass and a little harder to kick, but it's the same on both sides and everyone adjusts. In the stands, insulated pants and ski jackets are the norm, most topped off with a sponge cheesehead for a hat.

Despite the weather, or because of it, this is a magnificent game—not perfect but brilliant to behold.

On their first possession the Giants execute 14 plays consuming nearly 8 minutes before Lawrence Tynes kicks a field goal. While this is a good result, the opportunities missed by the Giants, opportunities to score touchdowns, become troubling.

Fans and players found themselevs in **frigid Green Bay** for the NFC Championship.

Captain for Life
When Harry Carson Speaks...

"Happiness," Harry Carson said, "is a warm locker room. A warm victorious locker room."

And he should know. The former linebacker and team captain was a key symbolic part of the Giants' team in Green Bay on January 20 for the NFC Championship Game, a game played in the third coldest conditions in NFL history. Carson, along with Lt. Col. Greg Gadson, was an honorary co-captain, chosen by Coach Tom Coughlin.

A war hero and a Hall-of-Famer—it had to be a good choice for the Giants.

"Nobody was cold on the bench it seemed," Carson recalled. "There was a whole lot of enthusiasm. I was cold, though."

But he stuck it out. "I wanted to encourage them," he said, "I wanted to help them live in the now and help the players understand the emotions of the day. The winner of this game would be the one who lasted the longest."

Carson's place in Giants history—as a 13-year star at linebacker, who played through some tough seasons and some great ones, including Super Bowl XXI—means the players paid attention.

On the sidelines, Carson recalled hearing players saying: Be cold the next day; be hurt the next day. "I was in awe of their spirit."

"We were well prepared on the sideline with heaters," Manning says when it's over. "I stood by them the whole game. I had big gloves around my hand. I kept my hand warm, that was the main thing."

For Eli, it is another game without turnovers—21 completions in 40 attempts and 251 yards. The only turnover by the Giants comes when R.W. McQuarters intercepts a Favre pass in the fourth quarter and then fumbles it back to the Packers on his return.

In the second quarter, the Giants move the ball well but again settle for a Tynes field goal. It's 6-0.

The Packers muff the next kickoff but recover the ball. They are starting from their own 10. On first down, the Packers' Donald Driver

Happy Kicker
Lawrence Tynes

LAWRENCE TYNES HAS A FINE SENSE OF HUMOR, surely a necessity for a field goal kicker.

In the Wild-Card playoff game against Tampa Bay, Tynes's second-half kickoff resulted in a fumble after a hit by the Giants' Tank Daniels. The loose ball bounced toward the kicker, who was "filling a lane," as he recalled. When Tynes went to grab the ball, he was wiped out by Buccaneers. "I did some kind of somersault," he recalled. "My friends found it funny to watch." Corey Webster finally recovered, and the Giants went on a five-minute drive that ended with a Tynes field goal.

Tynes said that, given the light practice schedule of a place-kicker, "Everyone wants to be a kicker during the week. But no one wants to do it on Sunday."

After missing two fourth-quarter kicks in the NFC Championship Game in frigid Green Bay, Tynes ran onto the field on his first chance in overtime of that game without waiting for Coach Coughlin's OK.

"I made a career decision," Tynes said.

Then he got serious and said, "It never even crossed my mind that I wouldn't make that one."

One fan he delighted a few days later was David Letterman, the host of The Late Show on CBS.

As Tynes and Letterman watched a videotape of the badly missed second kick, the guest said: "Right about there, I'm thinking what's it going to be like to live in Green Bay." Afterwards, Tynes recalled: "That got him cackling."

Shortly after Tynes joined the Giants in the spring of 2007, he met the former tight end Howard Cross who played for the team for 13 seasons and appeared in two Super Bowls.

"Hi," Tynes said, "I'm LT."

Cross looked at the 6-1, 200-pound kicker and said succinctly: "No, you're not." And then he greeted the new man as a mere mortal might expect to be greeted.

gets past Corey Webster, and Favre hits him in stride for a 90-yard touchdown play. The Giants have had the ball for 25 plays so far, the Packers for 14. Green Bay is leading. Late in the quarter, the Packers get a field goal, and it's 10-6 at the half.

In the locker room, "we talked about taking the opening kickoff and driving the ball and scoring," says Coughlin. "We knew we had to score touchdowns."

And on the first possession they do. Mixing runs and passes (and a fumble recovery by Kevin Boss), the Giants get a Jacobs touchdown and take the lead.

Back come the Packers. Favre's pass to Donald Lee puts them in front. The Giants are surely not done. Ahmad Bradshaw is in at running back and, after Manning's eight-yard completion to Plaxico Burress, runs the ball twice for 14 yards. A 23-yard pass to Toomer is followed by an eight-yarder, and then Bradshaw runs for the touchdown, creating another Giants lead.

When Mason Crosby kicks his second field goal early in the fourth quarter, the score is tied. What follows makes Giants fans cringe: Tynes misses a 43-yard field goal attempt after a five-minute drive. The Packers can't move the ball, and punt; the Giants do the same on their next possession. The Packers stall again and they punt it away with 2:30 to play.

McQuarters fumbles the punt, Green Bay nearly gets it, but Hixon saves his new team by covering the ball.

On first down from the Green Bay 48, Bradshaw goes off left guard for an apparent game-leading touchdown. But there's holding upfield and the play comes back. The drive goes on. When the Giants reach the Green Bay 18 with 5 seconds to play, Manning spikes the ball to stop the clock and bring Tynes on. A high snap, a hurried kick, a frigid ball, a slippery field, and the kick misses badly.

"It's like kicking cardboard," says Tynes.

Overtime and the Packers win the toss.

On second down, Favre hopes to connect with Driver, again matched against Webster, the cornerback enjoying postseason

Future Hall-of-Fame inductee **Brett Favre** leads the Packers out for overtime.

Hot in the cold: the Giants reach the Super Bowl on **Lawrence Tynes**'s 47-yard overtime field goal, shown splitting the uprights, opposite.

redemption. Favre is pressured on the play and Webster intercepts the pass. As the defensive back goes to the sidelines he hands the ball to Lt. Col. Gadson, sitting alongside the Giants bench with this son Jaelen.

"This is for you," Webster says to Gadson.

The Giants take over at the Packer 34. Two running plays gain five and then Eli throws an incompletion. Fourth down at the 29—a 47-yard field goal if Coughlin lets Tynes kick it. But he has no choice. Tynes is already on the field bringing his holder Jeff Feagles and the long snapper Jay Alford.

"I just ran on the field," says Tynes. "I knew it was going to be close to 50, but I knew I could get it there. I kind of made the decision for him."

Alford's snap is perfect, Feagles hold is perfect, and Tynes kick is perfect.

Tynes bolts for the locker room while his teammates dance and hug and shout on the field.

"I just wanted to get out of the cold," he says.

Eli Manning has had his third straight playoff game without a turnover. Plaxico Burress has 11 catches for 154 yards and a franchise postseason record. And the Giants have their 10th consecutive road win, the longest one-season streak in NFL history.

Outside the Giants locker room Olivia Manning sees her son and says quietly to him: "It's good to see you smiling, honey."

GIANTS 23 • PACKERS 20 • IN OVERTIME • (13-6)

This stunning team has beaten all the Sirens. In Greek mythology the Sirens are three dangerous women. For the Giants they are three dangerous quarterbacks—Jeff Garcia, Tony Romo and Brett Favre.

New England and Tom Brady have defeated San Diego in the AFC championship.

There's one to go.

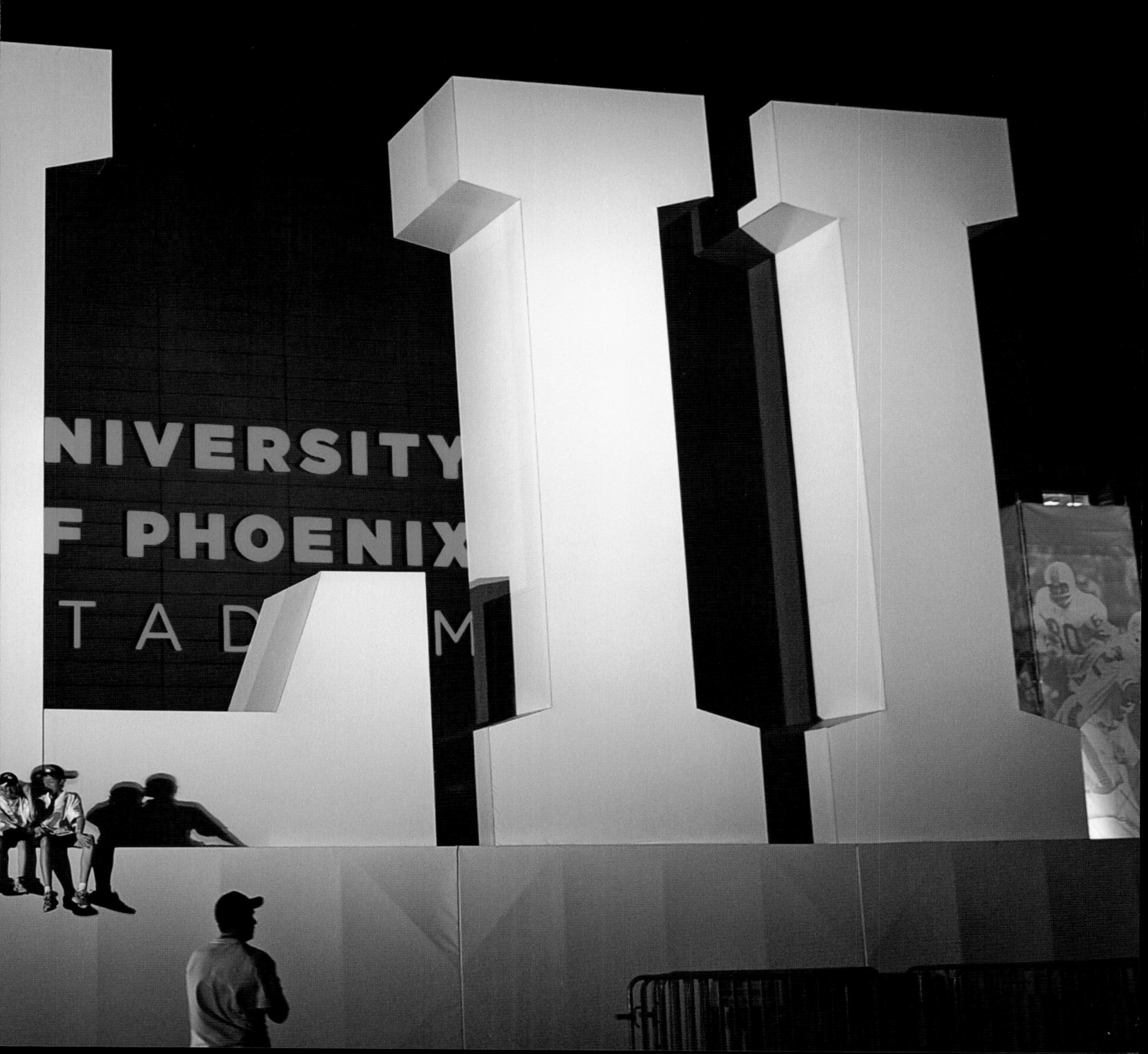
NIVERSITY
F PHOENIX
TAD M
80

"WHO SAW THIS COMING?" writes Harvey Araton in the *Times*. "Isn't the payoff more enjoyable when athletes surprise themselves, delight their fans and appear almost magically on the grand national stage?"

No one disagrees.

With two weeks between the conference championships and the Super Bowl, football steps aside for a few days so that New York can have a look at its new stars.

On the Monday after the big win, the players rest up, warm up, and some go dancing at a trendy club. On Tuesday morning, Gibril Wilson and Geoffrey Pope ring the bell to open trading on the New York Stock Exchange. On Tuesday evening, R.W. McQuarters, Aaron Ross, Plaxico Burress and Steve Smith give Knick fans something to cheer about at

Lawrence Tynes' appearance on *The Late Show With David Letterman* was as much about the two field goals he missed against the Packers as it was about the 47-yarder he successfully kicked in overtime to put the Giants into the Super Bowl.

ny FAN•POST

I thought the Giants had a decent shot to beat the Patriots and said so both in my game preview on my website and during radio interviews. The hosts of a Medford, Mass., radio station laughed at me when I said it would not surprise me if Manning won the game with a last-second touchdown drive. I was surprisingly confident. It was clear from the start that so were the Giants.

Eric Kennedy
Fredericksburg, VA

Madison Square Garden. On Wednesday, Lawrence Tynes, a guest on *The Late Show With David Letterman*, gives the host something to laugh about: "The first one looked like *I* kicked it," says Letterman, talking about the first of Tynes's two fourth-quarter misses against Green Bay.

Tynes replies, "No, no, I would say the second one probably looked like you would have kicked it"—the second having barely reached the goal line.

Not far away, another football player is trying to enjoy a few days in New York—Tom Brady. He is spotted near his supermodel girlfriend's Greenwich Village brownstone carrying flowers and wearing a protective boot over a walking cast on his sprained right ankle. The New York

Making Believers
The Media Reaction

MANY IN THE MEDIA WERE STUNNED as the 2007 New York Football Giants moved from Tampa to Dallas to Green Bay to Glendale. Here's some of what was said:

"What about Eli Manning winning three playoff games on the road, prevailing in minus-1 degree weather in Green Bay and leading the underdog Giants to the Super Bowl? My God, look at the previous sentence again! Just look at it!"
   – Bill Simmons, ESPN.com

"Raise your hand if you really think the San Diego Chargers with a hobbled quarterback, a hobbled running back and a hobbled tight end are going into Foxboro and beating the unbeaten New England Patriots. Raise the other hand if you think the gritty New York Giants with young Eli are walking into Green Bay, in what is supposed to be single-digit weather, and ending the made-for-TV movie that is the 2007 Packers, starring 57-year-old Brett Favre."
   – John Feinstein, *Washington Post*

"Beaten at Dallas and trounced by Green Bay, the New York Giants seemed headed to a lost season after only two games. Well, guess what? Eli Manning and the guys are a game away from the Super Bowl, following a path filled with vengeance."
   – Jaime Aron, *Dallas Morning News*

"At some point during the NFL postseason, most of America expected to see Tony Romo and Jessica Simpson—or least Brett Favre and the Green Bay Packers—taking on mighty New England in the Super Bowl. But Romo and the Dallas Cowboys have fallen, along with Favre and the Packers—both compliments of the New York Giants."
   – Jim Thomas, *St. Louis Post Dispatch*

Celebrity gossip and sportswriting converged when **Tom Brady**, above, was spotted in Manhattan wearing a protective boot on his right foot. **Eli**, meanwhile, tried to keep his mind on football. New York-native **Alicia Keys** (opposite) was part of the elaborate pregame show in Arizona.

media goes wild for this, and *Boston Globe* columnist Bob Ryan criticizes Brady's down-time destination.

Just some normal pre-Super Bowl stories.

By the time the teams get to Phoenix for Sunday's game, everyone is ready to return to football. But a story appears in the *Boston Herald* that the Patriots, whose unbeaten season has been dogged with reports of in-game videotaping of their opponents, taped the final practice of their Super Bowl XXXVI opponents, the St. Louis Rams, in 2002, in violation of NFL bylaws. And so it goes.

Just before leaving for Phoenix, Plaxico Burress gives a prediction to a *New York Post* reporter. "Are you ready to make history?" he is asked. "You better believe it," he responds. And then, asked for a prediction, he says, "23-17."

When Brady hears this on Tuesday in Arizona, he scoffs. "We're only going to score 17?"

During a session with his leadership council, Coughlin assigns

Pregame Chatter
The Art of the Prediction

EVERYBODY MAKES A SUPER BOWL PREDICTION. The Patriots did when they tried to copyright "19-0". New York did when, prior to the big game, the city began laying plans for a victory parade for the Giants. Even the Patriots' hometown newspaper The Boston Globe did, by talking about plans for an "instant" book when the Pats completed their history-making season.

It was Joe Namath who helped make the Super Bowl... well, super, when he "guaranteed" that his Jets would defeat the favored Baltimore Colts in Super Bowl III in 1969.

So why did so many get so upset when Plaxico Burress, at right, predicted his Giants team would win Super Bowl XLII by 23-17? He labeled it a prediction; in New England, it was seen as a guarantee.

"It's all entertainment; we're all having fun with it," Burress said. "Muhammad Ali made predictions and he

went out and got it done." One thing Burress wanted perfectly clear: "It wasn't a guarantee."

During the week before the game, a headline in The Boston Herald said: "Predictably, Plax Talks a Good Game."

Patriots safety Rodney Harrison was none too happy about it all: "You put a lot of pressure on yourself when you make comments like that. We just shut up and we play football. He'll have his opportunity to prove it on Sunday."

Giants co-captain Antonio Pierce had the final answer (or question in this case): "Are we supposed to say we're going to lose?"

responsibility for team fashion during the trip west to co-captain Antonio Pierce. His decision, knowing there will be many cameras recording their arrival, is that the team will wear all black. Almost everyone does.

Each day's focus is on Brady's ankle; on the Patriots' quest to go unbeaten; the Giants stunning appearance on this stage… and of course on Plaxico's prediction.

Coach Coughlin tries to accustom the players to a new schedule

Ready to rock: **Michael Strahan**, opposite, leads the Giants defense onto the field at the University of Phoenix Stadium.

Putting on the Game
It Doesn't Just Happen

EACH YEAR, THE NFL PUTS A NEW FIELD in the Super Bowl stadium. But for XLII, a new strategy was required.

The University of Phoenix Stadium in Glendale, Arizona, has a unique "tray" system for its field. The grass spends most of its time growing in the Arizona sunshine, properly watered and drained, while sitting in its portable tray in a parking area. On game day, the tray is rolled through doors on the south end of the facility and installed in about an hour. The system has worked very well in the 2-year-old facility.

But the Super Bowl presented unique problems.

"We trucked in sod in 19 refrigerated semis," said Frank Supovitz, the NFL's Senior VP of Events, who is responsible for all functional details. "The object was to lay the sod in the tray and keep it growing outside."

Outside, the grass can be kept healthy with sunshine, proper watering and good drainage. Inside, there is no sunshine, no watering system and no drainage. That's why the field usually goes in only on the day of the game, and only for a few hours.

But temporary stands had to be built to accommodate ticket buyers and those would block the tracks the tray rolls on. In addition, the tray's parking area was needed for broadcast and media centers.

So the field made its final entrance on Thursday, and the NFL worked to keep the grass thriving.

With a retractable roof, the question of whether the game would be played "outdoors" or "indoors" had to be answered. The coaches asked for 24 hours notice of the decision (to be made by NFL Commissioner Roger Goodell) so they could make adjustments.

"It had been cold with rain in Phoenix," recalled Supovitz. "So we recommended that the roof be closed. Better to close it and risk having made a mistake if no rain came."

The roof was closed on a cool, rainless night.

In the end, on the advice of NFL owners, the pregame schedule was adjusted to give the players the field closer to game time—after the pregame show rather than before. Previously, the players had had to leave the field at least an hour before the game.

And because the roof was closed, the halftime show had to change. You may have seen fireworks while Tom Petty performed but "to keep the smoke to a minimum," Supovitz recalled, "we scaled down 95 percent of the pyrotechnics."

built around three days of required media sessions. "What we've done is go from an early morning operation to practicing at game time," he says. "But about the middle of the day you start getting a little antsy, because we haven't met and we haven't practiced yet."

Finally, on game day, the slogan Coach used to start the season—the pregame advice of the great John Unitas—has stronger meaning:

"Talk is cheap. Play the game."

Super Bowl Sunday, February 3, 2008
Glendale, Arizona

The game starts perfectly for the Giants. They win the toss and Eli performs as if he's managing the two-minute drill. But the clock's running and the offense eats time and yardage. After two running plays, Manning connects with Burress for 14 yards.

Ahmad Bradshaw, above, gained eight yards over right tackle before being brought down at the New England 29 for a first down. This lengthy opening drive resulted in a 32-yard field goal by **Lawrence Tynes,** opposite.

The ankle problems remain (at one point this week a knee injury, caused by a fall in a shower, gave Burress the feeling that he would be unable to play). But he is out there.

Runs or passes work equally well, and the Giants have first and 10 on the Patriots 17, having converted four third downs on the way there. Then the drive stalls, and Lawrence Tynes kicks a field goal. But the drive has lasted 9 minutes 59 seconds, the longest in Super Bowl history.

The fans worry that, as in Green Bay, the team needs to get a touchdown after a drive like that. A field goal is not enough.

The Patriots take the kickoff, and their own first drive is as impressive as that of the Giants but more productive. In the regular season, Brady and his offense scored a league-record 589 points, and, after a long kickoff return by Laurence Maroney and 12 plays from

scrimmage, consuming more than five minutes, Maroney scores from a yard out and the Patriots lead 7-3.

If there is a positive note for the Giants, it's that during the drive they hit Brady twice as he released passes, and applied enough pressure that four of his throws were hurried. "We told the guys that even if he's released the ball, try to get a hit on him," says defensive coordinator Steve Spagnuolo. "And for every time I told the guys that, Strahan told them another four times."

The Giants start their next drive at their 40. The offense continues to be effective. The game so far has the feel of a high-scoring showdown. A long pass to Amani Toomer gives Big Blue a first down at the Patriot 19. After a penalty, Manning connects for a short gain with the little-used David Tyree. On third down from the 14, Manning's pass to Steve Smith bounces off the receiver and into the hands of the Patriots' Ellis Hobbs. Eli's streak without an interception is over.

With that turnover, the game changes from an offensive show to one having the longest scoreless streak ever in a Super Bowl.

The Patriots go three and out, stopped by Strahan and James Butler's tackle of Maroney on third down.

The Giants can't move either. Jeff Feagles booms a punt, and the Giants' defense takes over.

On second and 10, Kawika Mitchell sacks Brady. On the next play it's Justin Tuck's turn. The Patriots punt and the Giants mount a drive featuring the running of Brandon Jacobs and Ahmad Bradshaw. A fumble stalls the march even though possession is maintained. A

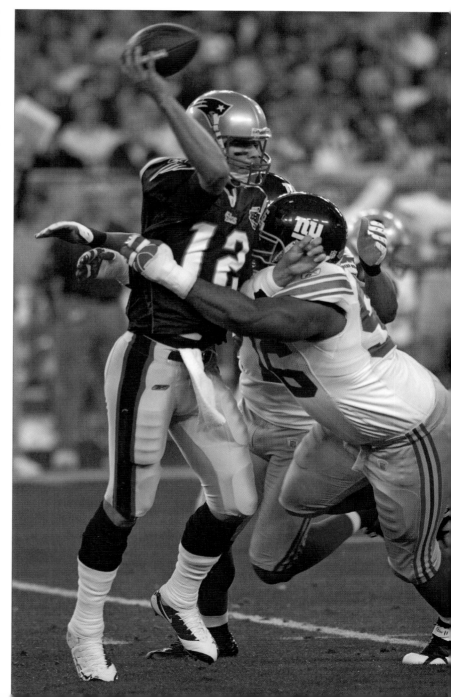

Mirroring the final regular-season meeting between the Giants and Patriots, New York continued to pressure **Tom Brady**, hurrying his release on numerous plays and sacking him five times by game's end.

Kawika Mitchell, opposite, sacked Tom Brady and then exhorts the crowd and his teammates to not let up.

Feagles punt puts the Patriots deep in their territory.

The Patriots begin to click. As if to show the Giants who the favored team really is, Brady connects on a third and 13 for 18 yards.

New England moves to the Giants' 44 with 22 seconds in the half. Then on first down, Justin Tuck breaks free for his second sack and Brady fumbles. Osi Umenyiora recovers.

The half ends with the Patriots still in the lead.

The Giants defense is dishing out more than the Patriots are used to getting.

"We felt like we could dominate them," Michael Strahan says. "We

Completing the Circle
Jeff Feagles

FOR PUNTER JEFF FEAGLES, the 2007 season brought his football life full circle. Feagles had spent much of the 2006 off-season trying to decide whether he wanted to return for his 19th NFL campaign or retire and spend more time at his home in the Phoenix area. Encouraged by his children, Feagles opted to come back and then stayed on to play a 20th season as well.

Twenty years after he boomed his first professional punt for the New England Patriots, he was in Arizona playing in his first Super Bowl against the New England Patriots.

"I'm a rookie again," said Feagles. "An old rookie. I definitely had my doubts about it ever happening. Now it's kind of like getting my cake and eating it, too."

His road was a long one; it covered five teams (New England, Philadelphia, Arizona, Seattle and the Giants) and saw him set a record for consecutive games played (320).

When Feagles does retire, it is his leg for which he will likely be most remembered. But to the 2007 Giants, Feagles's hands were just as important. Serving as the holder on converts and field goals, Feagles had the responsibility of working not just with new snappers (Jay Alford and Zak DeOssie) but with a new place kicker, Lawrence Tynes.

It may sound like a minor detail, but try to imagine what was going through Feagles's mind on that frigid night in Green Bay as he called for the snap, caught the ball, placed it and watched Lawrence Tynes send him to his first Super Bowl.

led the league in sacks, and when we get against the Patriots, we're supposed to not be able to pass rush? That's what we do."

Brady has a decent day statistically. By game's end he will have completed 29 of 48 for 266 yards and a touchdown. But he will have been sacked five times, knocked down or hit another 20. Spotted on the sidelines by a TV camera in mid-game, his face shows bewilderment at what is taking place.

"No one was going near him on the bench," one fan observed. "You heard the hits in the stands. You felt them."

Justin Tuck knows there's no reason to rejoice at halftime. "It's still Tom Brady out there and he's still good," he says.

As the second half begins, the teams try to find a way to get back to scoring.

Helped by a rare New York penalty, it looks as if the Patriots will do just that. They move downfield on seven plays but then stall and are about to punt. But as the teams line up, Giant special team player Chase Blackburn realizes the Giants have 12 men on the field and scurries off as Feagles punts. Patriots coach Bill Belichick spots him with one foot still on the field, and challenges the play. Replay confirms the challenge, a penalty is called and it's first down on the Giants 39. Momentum seems to have shifted.

On third down, Brady connects with Kevin Faulk, and it's first and 10 at the 28. A run for no gain, a pass for three, and on third down, Strahan breaks through and chases down Brady for a loss of six. On fourth and 13 at the 31—typically field goal range, but the Patriots choose to gamble—Brady throws incomplete, and the Giants take over.

Each team's next drive stalls, and the fourth quarter begins with the Giants at their own 20, first and 10.

The first down play—Manning to the rookie tight end Kevin Boss—works perfectly. "We were looking to create some kind of a void," says Coughlin, "and the ball was put in the perfect spot." The play gains 45 yards before Rodney Harrison brings Boss down.

A Giants running back from the early 70s, Bob Duhon, says to his son Chris as they watch in the stands: "We've got them. We're looking good right now."

Three Bradshaw runs and a pass to the rookie Steve Smith give the

Girbil Wilson and Antonio Pierce, opposite, combine to stop Kevin Faulk at the Giants 28 in the third quarter. The defense held and, in what would prove to be a turning point, the Patriots elected not to kick and turned the ball over on downs at the Giants 31-yard line.

Giants second down at the 5.

Manning throws short over the middle to an unexpected target, David Tyree, who catches the ball in the back center of the end zone. The scoring drought is over, ended by the native of Montclair, NJ. The Giants lead.

"I was pretty content when I caught the touchdown pass," Tyree says. "I thought, 'OK, Lord, thanks. Now let's get out of here with a win.'" But there is more in store for David Tyree.

On the next Giants series Manning and Burress fail to connect, although the receiver is wide open.

After another exchange of punts, the Patriots offense returns. They

go 80 yards in 12 plays as the Giants pass rush is stymied. With 2:45 to play, New England retakes the lead on a touchdown pass from Brady to Randy Moss. It's 14-10.

The Patriots kick off. Hixon gets the ball back only to the 17. First and 10. Two minutes 39 seconds to play. Eighty-three yards to go.

On the sidelines, the defense, so strong all game, chants "Believe".

Strahan turns it up a notch. "17-14! Believe it. Don't just say it, believe it!"

It's Eli Time.

"I'm glad we're down by 4," he would say later. "It means we have to go for a touchdown."

On first down, he passes to Amani Toomer for 11 and then throws two incompletes intended for Burress. On third down he connects with Toomer again but they're short by a yard. On television the announcers speculate that the Giants might punt and hope to get the ball back. No such thought occurs on the field, not with Brandon Jacobs in the backfield.

Steve Smith's fourth-quarter catch, opposite, was good for 17 yards and a first down on New England's 12 yard line. Eli capped the drive, above, with a five-yard strike to David Tyree for the score.

Jacobs bulls and then claws his way for two yards, extending his arm with the ball at the last moment to assure he's made the distance. First down.

Then Eli scrambles for five and the ball comes loose, but his knee has already touched, and he recovers anyway. On second down he throws to Tyree on the sideline. The ball tips off the hands of the Patriots' Asante Samuel and falls out of bounds.

"Richard Seymour was out there telling us, 'Hey, guys, get ready to

Scamble time: Manning, left, is stripped of the ball by **Adelios Thomas**, but the Giants retain possession and the quarterback gains a crucial five yards. A timeout and two plays later, **Eli** appears to be sacked, but shakes off several defenders, below, and throws downfield to **David Tyree** to complete what is soon hailed as the greatest play in Super Bowl history.

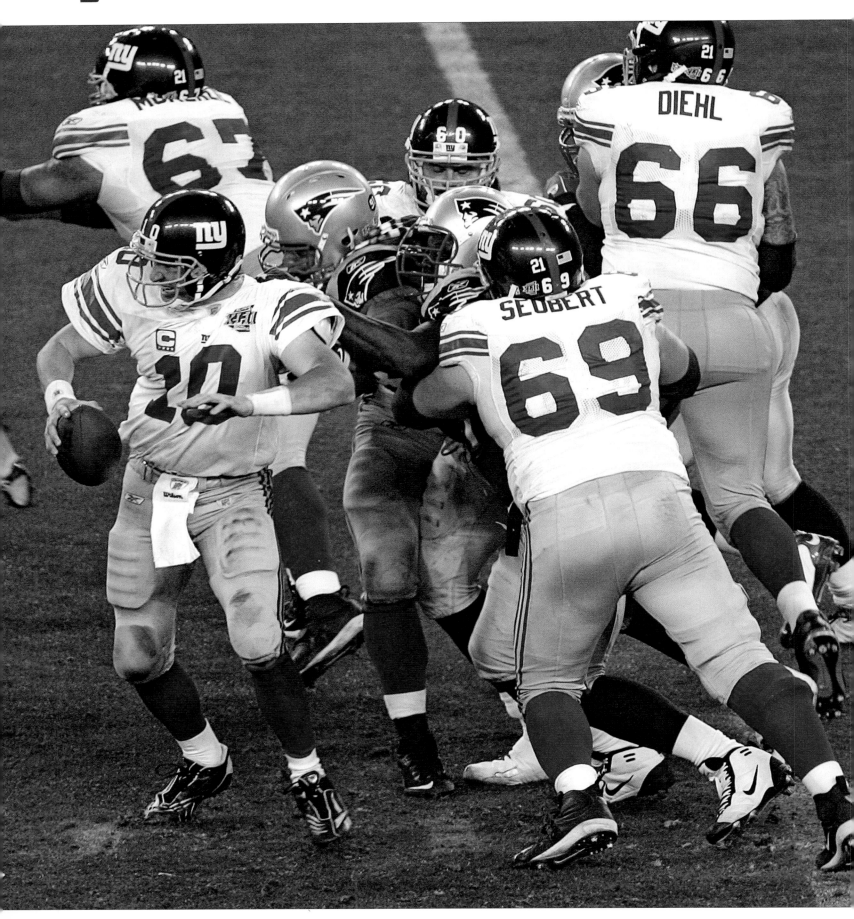

go home,'" says Toomer. "What's the sense in tempting fate like that?"

Third down and five from the Giants 44. Eli motions and jiggles and points as he awaits the shotgun snap. The Giants have four receivers in the formation—Burress and Tyree out wide and Steve Smith and Toomer in the slots. The protection breaks down quickly and Eli is about to be dropped. Somehow he escapes Richard Seymour and Jarvis Green's hands grabbing his jersey and recovers his balance as he stumbles from the scrum of bodies.

Down field the self-described "last guy in the read," Tyree, is running a deep post route. He turns, sees his quarterback in trouble and knows it's time he "found the void."

More views of **Eli's scramble** before finding **David Tyree** downfield. He keeps his feet moving and eventually breaks free.

"I felt them holding me," Manning says, "but I never felt anybody pull me to the ground. I stayed alive and I saw David in the middle of the field."

He launches a pass.

At the Patriots 25, Tyree gets ready. "I'm open but not for long." As Patriots safety Rodney Harrison closes in, Tyree leaps. At his highest point, he grabs the ball as Harrison "clobbers me." Tyree's left hand comes off the ball as he tries to control it with his right. The ball comes

David Tyree goes way, way up to haul in Eli's 32-yard pass. **Rodney Harrison** (37), above, begins to battle for the ball while both are still in the air.

Tyree's focus is solely on retaining possession. He pins the ball against his helmet as **Harrison** sets to slam him to the turf.

down on his helmet, his right hand on top of it as he heads to the ground.

"It wasn't luck," Tyree says. "Luck is finding a $50 bill on the ground." Harrison is not done as he tries to claw the ball out of Tyree's grip. But no use. "Now I know anything's possible," says Tyree.

Time-out New York.

It's first down and the Giants still have 24 yards to go with 59 seconds to play.

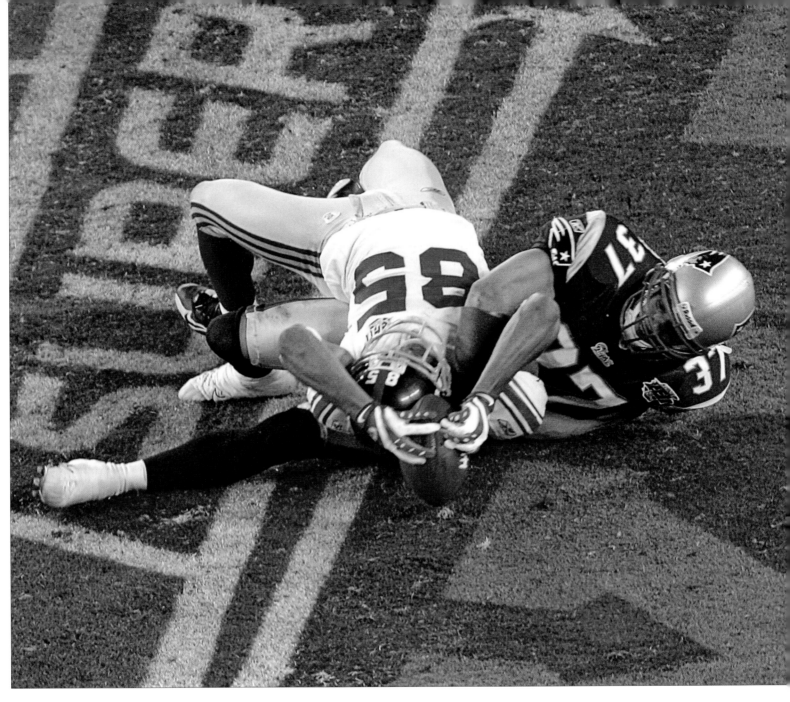

Adalius Thomas, who grew up and played football in the same tiny Alabama town as Justin Tuck, sacks Eli for a small loss.

Second down: Manning goes for his new favorite Tyree, but this time he throws incomplete.

Third down: Eli spots rookie Steve Smith on the right sideline and connects. But Smith, who stays on his feet, is short of the first down and needs to get out of bounds to stop the clock. He moves up field, gets the extra yards and goes out of bounds.

For a moment, **Tyree** is bent back over the Patriots strong safety. Battling, he prevents the point of the ball from striking the ground where it would likely be jarred loose, holding on to put the Giants in scoring position with just under a minute left in the fourth quarter.

Steve Smith, above, made this key third-down catch, tiptoeing his way to a first down before being pushed out of bounds, stopping the clock with 39 seconds left and the ball on the Patriots 13. This set the stage for **Eli** to loft a perfect pass to **Plaxico Burress** in the corner of the end zone, right and opposite, giving the Giants the lead with 29 seconds to play.

Thirty-nine seconds to play.

In the huddle, Eli calls "62 Café," knowing the Patriots will be blitzing. As he calls signals, he also knows that his best receiver, Burress, has not caught a pass since the game's opening series and that he'll be covered one-on-one. "That's a match-up we're going to take every time," he would say in retrospect.

The receiver, who for much of the season has spent practice studying because he was too injured to participate, runs a perfect route—a fake inside and then a fade into the end zone. He's alone, and Eli throws a perfect, high pass. "A rare spiral for me," he jokes.

"I'm just there thinking, 'C'mon down,'" Burress says. "I was watching my feet, to make sure they were in-bounds and everything." Turning his body back to the pass, he makes the catch.

Brady was sacked by **Jay Alford**, left, before attempting two deep passes to **Randy Moss** on third and fourth down. **Corey Webster**, above, breaks up the first. **Gibril Wilson**, the second.

After Tynes's extra point, the Giants lead by three points. There are 35 seconds to play.

The Patriots start from their 26. On first down Brady throws incomplete. On second, Jay Alford, the rookie defensive tackle, breaks through for the sack, the Giants fifth. Loss of 10.

On third down from the 16, Brady throws long down the left sideline—70 yards in the air—to Randy Moss. But Corey Webster breaks up the play. The Patriots have one more down.

Brady's last-chance throw goes almost as far as the previous one to the same receiver and falls incomplete. The Patriots have no more chances to save their unbeaten season.

Belichick runs for the dressing room, and the field is immediately covered with players and media and cameras.

But there's one more play for the Giants to run.

The field is quickly cleared, and Eli takes the snap and goes to one knee.

The New York Giants are the Super Bowl Champions.

"Every team is beatable, you know," Coughlin says.

SUPER BOWL XLII • GIANTS 17 • PATRIOTS 14 • (14-6)

Eli and elation after a kneel-down with one second left on the clock.

In his last talk with the Giants players in January 2007, the retiring General Manager Ernie Accorsi told the team: "Trust each other and be good teammates to one another. I believe there is a championship in this room."

In the summer at training camp, the new General Manager Jerry Reese said: "Why not us?"

And on a February night in a joyous locker room, team president John Mara says: "It's the greatest victory in the history of this franchise."

Career Capper
Strahan's Ultimate

WHICH IS WORSE, never getting to the Super Bowl, or getting there and being blasted off the field? According to Michael Strahan, it's absolutely the latter.

"I think last time we went we were almost thinking we won the Super Bowl just by getting there," Strahan said in describing the feeling prior to a 34-7 loss to the Baltimore Ravens in January 2001.

"But you learn that the ultimate thing is to win it," Strahan said before Super Bowl XLII. "So now I am happy, but I am not overjoyed and jumping up and down and all those things. I am focused on doing whatever we have to do to win."

For Strahan the day almost never came. He sat out of minicamps and training camp, trying to decide whether he wanted to return for his 15th season. Sitting home and watching the Giants make their Super Bowl run without him would have been a

nightmare, he said.

"If I quit, and the team went to the Super Bowl and won, I'd be holding somebody hostage until I got a ring, after all these years," Strahan quipped.

Defensive Coordinator Steve Spagnuolo isn't sure that the Giants would even have gotten the chance to win those rings without No. 92. "I frankly can't imagine making the run without him," Spagnuolo said. "I felt like he just got better and better as he went along. And he was as much a presence on the sidelines and in the meeting rooms as he was on the field."

Kevin Dockery gets a jump on his offseason reading.

ny FAN•POST

I had a ticket for Super Bowl XLII and I arrived at the stadium six hours early. Then I watched with the rest of the world for the first 57 minutes as the Giants stood "toe to toe" with what many had called the best football team of all-time. However, we were still down by 4 points. When Eli's final pass landed in Plaxico's arms for the game winning touchdown electricity went through University of Phoenix Stadium. All Giants fans exchanged high fives and hugged like we've known each other for 20 years even though this was the first, greatest and only game we would ever watch together. I had tears in my eyes—from happiness seeing my team win the Super Bowl, and from sadness, since my father who introduced me to NY Giants football had succumbed to ALS. I buried my dad with a picture of Eli Manning in his pocket. As I arrived home from the game that night, my five year old says "Daddy, give me a high five, we won the Super Bowl. When can we do that again"?

Adam Eagon
Scottsdale AZ

EPILOGUE
ECHOES FROM THE CANYON OF HEROES AND BEYOND

Previous page: Giants ownership and players receive the **Vince Lombardi Trophy** at the University of Phoenix Stadium. From left to right: Ann Mara, Terry Bradshaw, Eli Manning, Tom Coughlin, Jeff Feagles, John Mara and Steve Tisch.

Below: Though Wall Street hasn't used **tickertape** for years, New York proves it can stage the modern equivalent of a tickertape parade for their Super Bowl champions.

FROM A PARADE HONORING ADMIRAL GEORGE DEWEY, the hero of Manila Bay in 1899, through one for the New York Yankees in 2000, some 177 celebrations had taken place on the streets of Lower Manhattan called the Canyon of Heroes. Those parades honored, among others, astronauts, war heroes, presidents, politicians, foreign leaders, aviators, inventors, Olympic champions, baseball and hockey teams. But no football team had been celebrated until February 5, 2008 when the Super Bowl Champion New York Giants arrived.

The last time New York City hosted a parade in the Canyon was on October 30, 2000, for the World Series champion Yankees. Shortly afterwards, of course, lower Manhattan was devastated by the attacks of September 11, 2001. And while New York City, in general, and lower Manhattan, in particular, have made big comebacks, there hasn't been anything to celebrate.

Back in 1987, when the Giants won their first Super Bowl, New York

ny POSTGAME • FAN • POST • 1

Daniel Nixon, Ottawa, Ontario

I was raised to support only one team in my life—the Giants.

On Saturday night as the clock struck midnight and it became Super Bowl Sunday, I cut off all outside contact until the game was over.

After Brady found Moss, I was afraid that the end was near. "Don't worry, Eli will bring us back," were the words of my Dad. I'm not sure if he was trying to comfort us, bring our spirits up, or if he truly believed it. My Dad is 53 and has been a Giant fan all his life. I believed.

"Manning, lobs it, Burress! Alone! TOUCHDOWN NEW YORK!!"

Sweetest words I have ever heard.

Mark Machalek, Owego, NY

The earliest memory I have is sitting with my father on Sunday in his big red chair watching the Giants, always with a package of Genoa salami from Andy Wahila's Meat Market to snack on. Through years of lousy football he'd call it his good luck charm.

Dad passed away in 2002. As his heart failed him the last week of his life, he wore his newest Giant sweatshirt to keep warm.

I watched Super Bowl XLII with my 2-year-old daughter Hannah—she is dressed in her toddler Giants outfit. Among the words she has learned are "Giants" and "Shalami". Grandpa would have loved her. The good luck Genoa salami is present along with some new good luck items added during the playoff run—my Giants slippers, a gift from my son Jordan. Dad's sweatshirt drapes the couch.

Jordan calls many times during the game. Hannah jumps and shouts with me at every turn, and by the last few minutes I have lost my voice, my daughter is in a toddler tizzy, Jordan is yelling in the phone and my wife Sue thinks I have lost my mind.

Bruce Gilbert, Sedona, AZ

My friend Ed and I were still delirious with joy when we ventured out for breakfast the day after our stunning upset.. We were wearing our Super Bowl Champions Locker Room Hat and T-shirt. I live in Sedona, Arizona, a most magnificent and breathtakingly beautiful city, but no one seems to know much about sports. Recognizing the shape of a football would be a monumental feat for many.

So when Ed and I walked in to a favorite restaurant, the Coffeepot, with our Giants' paraphernalia, all the diners erupted with cheers and applause. It was awesome.

Bob Schinder, Forked River, NJ

On December 29, 2007, I had a hard time watching the Giants game against the Patriots. That day was the day my son Joseph Robert was born. It had been a very long delivery and I caught that game very tired and weary.

By the time the Giants went to Tampa Bay I had my new good luck charm by my side in his Giants outfit, just as he was for every playoff game and the Super Bowl. The Giants obviously did not lose a game with him in it.

The lucky outfit now is in a frame on the wall of my Giants shrine, just like an autographed jersey. When Joey gets older I can tell him how he may have had a little something to do with the Giants winning every game after he was born back in 2008.

Paul Machemer, Yardley, PA

I have had a commitment to the Giants since Pat Summerall's kick sailed though the snow and goal posts in 1958. This season in December my daughter in London was becoming serious about a young man. I needed to meet him. My wife and I scheduled a long weekend during the first weekend in February. My wife made the necessary reservations and then I double-clutched: Super Bowl weekend.

"No problem," I thought. "The Giants won't be playing."

Super Bowl weekend I'm in London, to meet some guy. At least the game is on the telly, if my hotel has the right channels. It does! International feed, different announcers, no commercials. Slowly the commentary changes from a coronation of the Patriots to begrudging respect for the Giants.

As Plaxico safely cradles the ball I'm nearly delirious. But Brady's got time. And the telly turns off, all by itself. I get it on again! Brady rolls right, and the telly again turns off. I get it going again. Fourth down incomplete. Eli takes a knee and the game's over.

I've got to be quiet. It's four in the morning!

Two weeks later, my daughter broke up with the guy.

Mayor Ed Koch vetoed the idea of a parade since the Giants play in New Jersey. After winning Super Bowl XXV in 1991, the Giants declined the offered honor, as the Gulf War had only recently begun, and a celebration was seen as inappropriate.

But now in 2008, New York Mayor Michael Bloomberg has made it crystal clear that the Giants represent his city, as they do the entire New York Metropolitan area. With fans from far beyond those limits, they surely represent even more.

So the champions of Super Bowl XLII, the Giants players, coaches and management stared in awe at the crowds that lined the streets around lower Broadway. Those in the throng and in the surrounding buildings shouted their love.

ny POSTGAME•FAN•POST•2

Christopher Richmond, North Bennington, VT

A 'fidian' is a person lacking in faith. It describes me and so many other Giants fans of a certain age. Growing up with the Giants through the Dark Ages, a certain expectation of disappointment frequently developed.

Throughout the playoffs I was expecting the worst and was delighted by success. Of course we could win if everything went right, but when does that ever happen?

At halftime of the Super Bowl I recall thinking the Giants were doing what they needed in order to have a chance. Deep into the second half I had this nagging belief that they could actually win! Being a good fidian I kept these thoughts well buried and as the Patriots drove down the field for their go-ahead score that flame of hope flickered to an ember, only to be revived by the heroic efforts of Manning and Tyree. Once that completion was made I said out loud, "My God, we could actually win this!" and by saying it, it became real. As the final seconds ticked away I turned from the television to my wife, sitting calmly in her chair, and saw her mouthing the words I had heard her say so many times that season,

"Oh ye, of little faith..."

Maybe a little faith isn't such a bad thing after all.

Steven Silfen, Randallstown, MD

For the past 15 years, Bob Bennett religiously watched and attended Giant games with me. He would go to training camp, to games at Giants Stadium and watch games at my house in Maryland.

In November, Bob needed to have back surgery. The night he was released from hospital, he suffered an apparent heart attack and passed away. As Bob had requested there was no funeral, however a party of remembrance was held celebrating his life. His wife Linda called me up to let me know that she had gotten a condolence letter from Coach Tom Coughlin who had been made aware of her husband's death through posts on Big Blue Interactive.

At the party Linda requested that Hope Johnson, myself and several of Bob's Giants fan friends take some of his ashes and sprinkle them on the parking lot, on the field, and at his seat at Giants Stadium.

We did this over several games but the Giants always seemed to lose when we did.

After the Super Bowl, I read that one of the Maras thought he saw someone throwing ashes on the field between the third and fourth quarter. I immediately called Hope and sure enough...

Sue Forestiero, Levittown, NY

I was born a Giant fan, thanks to a Dad who had the foresight in 1946 to get season tickets at the Polo Grounds. My mother recalls the prenuptial agreement she entered into just before their marriage in 1954—"even if we cannot put food on the table, we are not getting rid of the Giant tickets." My brother and I now attend games the way my parents once did. And like many fans, superstition is a huge part of my life. If the team is on a winning streak, you don't change anything.

We were invited to a friend's house to watch the Tampa Bay playoff on the friend's high definition TV. When the Giants won, we knew we had to keep going back, Dallas, Green Bay...and, of course, the Super Bowl.

We alienated more than a few friends who heard about our Super Bowl party and wanted to come. Sorry. Absolutely not. A serious, football watching, Giants Super Bowl experience. Same people, same seats, same food. We had to add a bucket in front of my brother who thought he was going to get sick when the Patriots got the ball back with 35 seconds left, but other than that nothing changed.

Lyle Silverman, Roseland, NJ

A routine medical procedure for mom was scheduled December 21, the day after I got back from school. She told me everything was fine. The surgery seemed to last forever and something did not seem right. The surgeon finally appeared and took my brothers, my stepfather and me into this tiny consultation room and said:

"Well, this is how we treat this type of Cancer."

My Mom. The strongest woman I know. After all she has been through and the great job she did raising her four children basically on her own, I could not fathom her not being by my side.

She taught me my Giants love, she was involved in all of our athletic pursuits. So together we watched and relished as the Giants clinched in Buffalo and then marched through the playoffs.

The miracle finish in Green Bay led to two of the longest weeks in my life. My brother and I turned down a chance to go to the game so that we could watch it with our mom. We knew that was the right thing to do. We were rewarded when...

"Manning, lobs it... Burress ALONE... TOUCHDOWN NEW YORK!!!!!"

My brother and I went absolutely wild, chest bumping, screaming, my sister jumping up and down. And then I looked back at my mom, on the couch with the biggest smile you could imagine.

The parade began at Bowling Green, near the tip of Manhattan Island, and by the time it ended, a mile away, with a City Hall ceremony, the love was permanent and everlasting. On the way the players passed hundreds of thousands of well-wishers, many holding signs such as "Tyree: Use Your Head," "18-1," and "True Blue".

"That's the best thing I've ever experienced in this city," said the hero of the victory over Green Bay, Lawrence Tynes. "I mean you saw grown men crying as we went by. I'm from a town of 8,000 in Florida. To see that many people cheering for you—it was something."

Tynes shared a float with punter Jeff Feagles, as the players were grouped by their team units—offensive line, linebackers, kickers and so forth.

One float carried a defensive end and a quarterback, along with a head coach, a general manager, a mayor and a special trophy. Michael Strahan, Eli Manning, Coach Tom Coughlin and Mayor Bloomberg took turns waving the Vince Lombardi Trophy to thunderous cheers and tons of shredded paper.

From his spot on that float, General Manager Jerry Reese was overwhelmed. "I really didn't know what to expect," he said. "And it just kept getting better."

At City Hall, Mayor Bloomberg played the happy host, and the fans heard from some of their favorites.

"I've had goose-bumps so many times in the last week that I'm starting to think it's normal," said Coughlin. "That show of loyalty and response to our championship season was something we'll remember the rest of our lives.

"This group of young men behind me, the 2007 New York Giants, displayed great character throughout the season—they epitomized the meaning of the word team. I told the coaches and players this morning that I wanted them to say as many times as they could in the next two weeks: 'The New York Giants, the 2007 Champions of the World.'"

Team president John Mara, whose grandfather Tim founded the Giants in 1925, and whose father Wellington ran the franchise for more than 70 years, said, "I can't tell you how proud the entire Giant organization is to represent the great city and state of New York and the great state of New Jersey. We are very proud to bring home the first championship to this city since the attacks of September 11, 2001. And we are very proud that it is our former team captain George Martin who is currently walking across America to raise awareness and funds to support the medical needs of the first responders of September 11.

"I can think of no better gift to give the greatest city in the world

Michael Strahan, **Coach Coughlin** and **Eli** join a trophy-hoisting **Mayor Bloomberg** on a parade float in Manhattan. Team President **John Mara**, below left, expressed the organization's joy at representing its great fans. Chairman **Steve Tisch**, below right, called the Giants, "America's Dream."

and the most loyal fans in the world than the most coveted trophy in all of sports, the Vince Lombardi Super Bowl Trophy."

Chairman and co-owner Steve Tisch recalled one of his team's rivals when he proclaimed that if the Dallas Cowboys could call themselves "America's Team," the Giants were now, "America's Dream."

Michael Strahan stood up to chants of "One more year!"

He said, "I know it's raining—everybody's getting wet. But this is New York, we're New Yorkers, we suck it up.

"In my 15 years with the Giants, I've played with some great teams, great players and coaches, but I've never ever played with a bigger group of goof balls than this group here. And you know what? We won the Super Bowl!

"Thank you to New York City for having us, and when I say New York City I mean New Jersey, Connecticut, the tri-state, the world, whoever's a Giant fan."

At this point the "one-more-year" chant rose again.

"One more year," responded Strahan. "We'll see! … I have a tradition with the guys. Whenever I'm talking, trying to give them a pep rally speech, they yell at me like they're doing right now, 'What are we gonna do?' And the answer is, 'We're gonna stomp you out!' That's what we call the family circle. Now everybody here, we're all in the family circle. And when I'm jumping up and down and I'm slamming my foot, we're stomping you out. We went on the road and we stomped out 11 straight. So we would like to extend this to every other team in the NFL, in particular the last team we defeated, the New England Patriots.

"We stomped you out!"

When he showed the audience how, they loved it.

A tough act to follow, and Eli Manning had the spot.

"I told Michael I wanted to talk first because I knew I couldn't compete with what he just did. I can't do the stomp. On behalf of the team I just want to tell you all how proud we are to bring a championship back to New York City. It's been an honor to play with this group of guys. We've had our ups, we've had our downs, but everything that we've gone through this season has made it so special. It's been an unbelievable journey, and I would not trade any moment for this moment right here standing up here in this city."

And then it was off to Giants Stadium.

With some 30,000 people in the stands and the Lombardi Trophy on display, the greeting was just as boisterous.

The players got a little more animated. They were 'home' after all.

Plaxico Burress gave his trademark deep bow to the crowd; David Tyree held a football against his head; Antonio Pierce led the "one-more-year" chant aimed at Michael Strahan.

Happy, happy day. Everyone from **firefighters**, opposite, to linbackers **Chase Blackburn** and **Reggie Torbor**, below, was in full party mode.

Some **young Giants fans** *did* go to school on parade day.

Steve Tisch explained the lesson of the Giants' victory: "Never challenge an underdog to a fight, because you're going to lose."

John Mara said: "When we pulled into this parking lot I was reminded that there is no place like home."

Manning, who may have heard some boos as the team struggled at home during the season, looked at the crowd and said: "It's good to get some cheers in Giants Stadium."

And the day was done.

The offseason began for the Giants as they left the Stadium. The Giants' remarkable run, along with the Patriots' attempt at perfection, had attracted a Super-Bowl-record television audience of 97.5 million in the United States, the second-most-watched program in history, behind the final episode of *M*A*S*H*.

The players made the rounds of the network talk shows. Eli Manning appeared on *The Late Show With David Letterman*, where the host said: "I can't thank you enough."

Michael Strahan was a guest on *Late Night with Conan O'Brien*.

David Tyree was probably busiest (see what a miracle catch can do?), appearing on several ESPN programs on both coasts and on *Jimmy Kimmel Live!* and *The Ellen DeGeneres Show*.

Everyone wanted a piece of this remarkable team achievement.

In late April, the team paid a visit to Washington, where the Giants spent part of the day visiting injured soldiers at Walter Reed Army Medical Center. At a White House ceremony with President George W. Bush, Lt. Col. Greg Gadson, the Giants inspiration, stood in the front row on his prosthetic legs and crutches and heard praise from his Commander-in-Chief:

"He's got the Purple Heart and three Bronze Stars," the President said. "And now he's got a Super Bowl ring minted for a true giant."

After being thanked by Coach Coughlin, the President received an autographed football from Eli Manning—and from Amani Toomer, a white road jersey, naturally.

"Once in a lifetime," Coughlin said later, adding: "Hopefully, more than that for us."

And now there was work to be done. Another season was approaching.

With 30,000 fans cheering them on at Giants Stadium, **Brandon Jacobs**, left, and **Plaxico Burress**, right, help **David Tyree** reenact his extraordinary catch.

NEW YORK GIANTS
GAME RESULTS • 2007

KEY TO ABBREVIATIONS: W/L – Win or Loss ; NYG Score – Giants score; Opp Score – Opponents score. OFFENSE: 1stD – First Downs made; TotYd – Total yards gained; PassY – Passing yards gained; RushY – Rushing yards gained; TO - Turnovers committed. DEFENSE: 1stD – First Downs allowed; TotYd - Total yards allowed; PassY – Passing yards allowed; RushY – Rushing yards allowed; TO – Turnovers forced. @ – Road game; N – Super Bowl played at Neutral site.

Week	Day	Date	W/L	Record	Opponent	NYG Score	Opp Score	OFFENSE 1stD	TotYd	PassY	RushY	TO	DEFENSE 1stD	TotYd	PassY	RushY	TO
REGULAR SEASON																	
1	Sun.	Sept. 9	L	0–1	@ Dallas Cowboys	35	45	22	438	314	124	1	21	478	336	142	2
2	Sun.	Sept. 16	L	0–2	Green Bay Packers	13	35	20	325	231	94	2	25	368	285	83	1
3	Sun.	Sept. 23	W	1–2	@ Washington Redskins	24	17	19	315	219	96	3	14	260	178	82	1
4	Sun.	Sept. 30	W	2–2	Philadelphia Eagles	16	3	16	212	129	83	1	16	190	76	114	1
5	Sun.	Oct. 7	W	3–2	New York Jets	35	24	21	374	186	188	2	16	277	222	55	3
6	Mon.	Oct. 15	W	4–2	@ Atlanta Falcons	31	10	28	491	303	188	3	14	284	181	103	1
7	Sun.	Oct. 21	W	5–2	San Francisco 49ers	33	15	21	279	139	140	1	20	267	164	103	4
8	Sun.	Oct. 28	W	6–2	@ Miami Dolphins	13	10	19	238	49	189	1	18	245	119	126	2
9					*bye week*												
10	Sun.	Nov. 11	L	6–3	Dallas Cowboys	20	31	23	300	194	106	2	19	323	243	80	1
11	Sun.	Nov. 18	W	7–3	@ Detroit Lions	16	10	19	341	269	72	2	17	376	351	25	4
12	Sun.	Nov. 25	L	7–4	Minnesota Vikings	17	41	18	309	234	75	4	15	251	124	127	0
13	Sun.	Dec. 2	W	8–4	@ Chicago Bears	21	16	24	356	181	175	4	18	312	244	68	0
14	Sun.	Dec. 9	W	9–4	@ Philadelphia Eagles	16	13	15	318	207	111	2	18	306	165	141	1
15	Sun.	Dec. 16	L	9–5	Washington Redskins	10	22	20	307	168	139	1	14	309	156	153	0
16	Sun.	Dec. 23	W	10–5	@ Buffalo Bills	38	21	17	383	94	289	4	16	244	127	117	4
17	Sat.	Dec. 29	L	10–6	New England Patriots	35	38	19	316	237	79	1	27	390	346	44	0
PLAYOFFS																	
WildCard	Sun.	Jan. 6	W	11–6	@ Tampa Bay Buccaneers	24	14	16	277	177	100	0	20	271	202	69	3
Division	Sun.	Jan. 13	W	12–6	@ Dallas Cowboys	21	17	16	230	140	90	0	23	336	182	154	1
ConfChamp	Sun.	Jan. 20	W	13–6	@ Green Bay Packers	23	20	24	377	243	134	1	13	264	236	28	2
SuperBowl	Sun.	Feb. 3	W	14–6	N New England Patriots	17	14	17	338	247	91	1	22	274	229	45	1

NEW YORK GIANTS ROSTER • 2007

KEY TO ABBREVIATIONS: Pos – Position, G – Games played, GS – Games started, WT – Weight, Ht – Height, Yrs – Years in NFL, R – Rookie.

#	Name	Age	Pos	G	GS	Wt	Ht	College/University	Birth Date	Yrs	Drafted (team/round/year)
93	Jay Alford	24	DT	16	0	280	6-2	Penn State	5/28/83	R	New York Giants/3rd/81st pick/2007
95	Adrian Awasom	24	DE	2	0	275	6-5	North Texas	10/25/83	2	
57	Chase Blackburn	24	LB	16	0	247	6-3	Akron	6/10/83	2	
77	Kevin Boothe	24	T	1	0	300	6-5	Cornell	7/5/83	1	Oakland Raiders/6th/176th pick/2006
89	Kevin Boss	23	TE	13	2	255	6-7	Western Oregon	1/11/84	R	New York Giants/5th/153rd pick/2007
44	Ahmad Bradshaw	21	RB	12	0	195	5-11	Marshall	3/19/86	R	New York Giants/7th/250th pick/2007
17	Plaxico Burress	30	WR	16	16	226	6-5	Michigan State	8/12/77	7	Pittsburgh Steelers/1st/8th pick/2000
37	James Butler	25	DB	13	12	210	6-3	Georgia Tech	9/7/82	2	
96	Barry Cofield	23	DT	16	15	305	6-3	Northwestern	6/7/85	R	New York Giants/4th/124th pick/2006
30	Craig Dahl	22	DB	9	2	207	6-1	North Dakota State	12/27/81	1	
52	Tank Daniels	26	LB	4	0	248	6-3	Harding	3/28/75	8	
99	Russell Davis	32	DT-DE	11	0	310	6-4	North Carolina	5/24/84	R	Chicago Bears/2nd/48th pick/1999
51	Zak DeOssie	23	LB	16	0	245	6-4	Brown	9/15/80	4	New York Giants/4th/116th pick/2007
66	David Diehl	27	G-T	16	16	315	6-5	Illinois	1/8/84	1	New York Giants/5th/160th pick/2003
35	Kevin Dockery	23	DB	13	6	188	5-8	Mississippi State	7/25/82	R	
24	Robert Douglas	25	RB	1	0	237	6-1	Memphis	8/21/78	6	Detroit Lions/3rd/81st pick/2000
22	Reuben Droughns	29	RB	16	1	207	5-11	Oregon	3/7/66	19	
18	Jeff Feagles	41	P	16	0	215	6-1	Miami (FL)	8/27/81	2	St. Louis Rams/7th/251st pick/2005
39	Madison Hedgecock	26	FB	15	9	266	6-3	North Carolina	10/8/84	R	Denver Broncos/4th/130th pick/2006
87	Domenik Hixon	23	WR	12	1	192	6-2	Akron	7/6/82	2	New York Giants/4th/110th pick/2005
27	Brandon Jacobs	25	RB	11	9	256	6-4	Southern Illinois	5/9/84	R	New York Giants/7th/224th pick/2007
20	Michael Johnson	23	DB	16	5	205	6-3	Arizona	3/8/83	1	New York Giants/1st/32nd pick/2006
97	Mathias Kiwanuka	24	LB	10	9	260	6-5	Boston College	2/14/81	1	
13	Jared Lorenzen	26	QB	2	0	275	6-4	Kentucky	4/23/74	10	Miami Dolphins/2nd/44th pick/1997
29	Sam Madison	33	DB	16	15	185	5-11	Louisville	1/3/81	3	San Diego Chargers/1st/1st pick/2004
10	Eli Manning	26	QB	16	16	218	6-4	Mississippi	10/9/83	R	
88	Michael Matthews	24	TE	16	6	270	6-4	Georgia Tech	5/24/79	6	New York Jets/3rd/79th pick/2001
67	Kareem McKenzie	28	T	16	16	327	6-6	Penn State	12/21/76	9	San Francisco 49ers/1st/28th pick/1998
25	R.W. McQuarters	31	DB	16	2	198	5-10	Oklahoma State	10/10/79	4	Kansas City Chiefs/2nd/47th pick/2003
55	Kawika Mitchell	28	LB	16	16	253	6-1	Georgia, S. Florida	1/20/83	R	
19	Anthony Mix	24	WR	4	0	235	6-5	Auburn	12/28/83	1	New York Giants/2nd/44th pick/2006
83	Sinorice Moss	24	WR	13	2	185	5-8	Miami (FL)	6/23/77	7	
60	Shaun O'Hara	30	G-C	16	16	306	6-3	Rutgers	12/31/77	7	New England/7th/239th pick/2000
36	Patrick Pass	30	FB	1	0	217	5-10	Georgia	10/26/78	6	
58	Antonio Pierce	29	LB	16	16	240	6-1	Arizona	3/25/77	7	Minnesota Vikings/2nd/55th pick/2000
98	Fred Robbins	30	DT	16	15	325	6-4	Wake Forest	9/15/82	R	New York Giants/1st/20th pick/2007
31	Aaron Ross	25	DB	15	9	193	6-1	Texas	6/11/76	7	Miami Dolphins/3rd/72nd pick/1999
65	Grey Ruegamer	31	C-G	16	0	310	6-4	Arizona State	3/30/79	6	
69	Rich Seubert	28	G	16	16	305	6-5	Western Illinois	8/18/80	5	New York Giants/1st/14th pick/2002
80	Jeremy Shockey	27	TE	14	14	253	6-5	Miami (FL)	5/6/85	R	New York Giants/2nd/51st pick/2007
12	Steve Smith	22	WR	5	0	195	6-0	USC	1/8/82	3	New York Giants/2nd/34th pick/2004
76	Chris Snee	25	G	16	16	314	6-3	Boston College	11/21/71	14	New York Giants/2nd/40th pick/1993
92	Michael Strahan	36	DE	16	15	275	6-5	Texas Southern	5/19/81	R	Green Bay/7th/253rd pick/2006
71	Dave Tollefson	26	DE	6	0	263	6-4		9/8/74	11	New York Giants/2nd/34th pick/1996
81	Amani Toomer	33	WR	16	15	208	6-3	Michigan	1/25/81	3	New York Giants/4th/97th pick/2004
53	Reggie Torbor	26	LB	16	5	254	6-2	Auburn	3/29/83	2	New York Giants/3rd/74th pick/2005
91	Justin Tuck	24	DE	16	2	268	6-5	Notre Dame	5/3/78	3	
9	Lawrence Tynes	29	K	16	0	202	6-1	Troy State	1/3/80	4	New York Giants/6th/211th pick/2003
85	David Tyree	27	WR	12	0	205	6-0	Syracuse	11/16/80	4	New York Giants/2nd/56th pick/2003
72	Osi Umenyiora	27	DE	16	16	280	6-3	Troy State	8/30/80	3	New York Jets/7th/235th pick/2004
34	Derrick Ward	27	RB	8	5	233	5-11	Fresno St.,Ottawa (KS)	2/10/85	R	
26	Danny Ware	22	RB	1	0	225	6-1	Georgia	3/2/82	2	New York Giants/2nd/43rd pick/2005
23	Corey Webster	25	DB	14	3	204	6-0	LSU	5/21/83	1	New York Giants/4th/129th pick/2006
79	Guy Whimper	24	DE	16	0	278	6-5	East Carolina	4/5/83	1	New York Giants/3rd/96th pick/2006
59	Gerris Wilkinson	24	LB	13	0	240	6-3	Georgia Tech	11/12/81	3	New York Giants/5th/136th pick/2004
28	Gibril Wilson	26	DB	13	13	197	6-0	Tennessee	2/14/76	7	
2	Anthony Wright	31	QB	4	0	211	6-1	South Carolina	4/13/84	2	Miami Dolphins/5th/1st pick/2005 Supp
75	Manuel Wright	23	DT	6	0	329	6-6	USC			
	Team Averages	**26.4**				**246.7**	**6-2.4**			**3.4**	

SUPER BOWL XLII PLAY-BY-PLAY

1st Quarter

Down/ Yds.To Go	Ball On	Time	Decription of Play – (Tackle by), [Pressure by]

New York Giants at 15:00

KICKOFF			3-S.Gostkowski kicks 72 yards from NE 30 to NYG -2. 87-D.Hixon to NYG 23 for 25 yards (58-P.Woods, 52-E.Alexander).
1-10	NYG 23	14:55	27-B.Jacobs left tackle to NYG 26 for 3 yards (96-A.Thomas).
2-7	NYG 26	14:14	27-B.Jacobs up the middle to NYG 28 for 2 yards (75-V.Wilfork, 94-T.Warren).
3-5	NYG 28	13:32	(Shotgun) 10-E.Manning pass short middle to 17-P.Burress to NYG 42 for 14 yards (36-J.Sanders).
1-10	NYG 42	12:53	10-E.Manning pass short left to 39-M.Hedgecock to NYG 45 for 3 yards (55-J.Seau).
2-7	NYG 45	12:03	27-B.Jacobs right tackle to NYG 46 for 1 yard (94-T.Warren).
3-6	NYG 46	11:17	(Shotgun) 10-E.Manning pass short left to 12-S.Smith to NE 46 for 8 yards (37-R.Harrison). NE-21-R.Gay was injured during the play.
1-10	NE 46	10:32	27-B.Jacobs left tackle to NE 39 for 7 yards (36-J.Sanders, 94-T.Warren).
2-3	NE 39	9:49	44-A.Bradshaw right guard to NE 37 for 2 yards (37-R.Harrison).
3-1	NE 37	9:01	44-A.Bradshaw right tackle to NE 29 for 8 yards (94-T.Warren, 75-V.Wilfork).
1-10	NE 29	8:17	10-E.Manning pass incomplete short left to 89-K.Boss.
2-10	NE 29	8:11	27-B.Jacobs right tackle to NE 26 for 3 yards (94-T.Warren, 50-M.Vrabel).
3-7	NE 26	7:27	(Shotgun) 10-E.Manning pass short middle to 12-S.Smith to NE 17 for 9 yards (50-M.Vrabel), [26-E.Wilson].
1-10	NE 17	6:41	(Shotgun) 10-E.Manning pass incomplete deep middle to 17-P.Burress (27-E.Hobbs).
2-10	NE 17	6:35	(Shotgun) 27-B.Jacobs left end to NE 18 for -1 yards (96-A.Thomas, 27-E.Hobbs).
3-11	NE 18	5:47	(Shotgun) 10-E.Manning pass short left to 12-S.Smith to NE 14 for 4 yards (37-R.Harrison).
4-7	NE 14	5:06	9-L.Tynes 32 yard **FIELD GOAL** is **GOOD**, Center-93-J.Alford, Holder-18-J.Feagles.

Super Bowl record: Longest drive (9:59).

NYG 3   NE 0   Plays: 16   Possession: 9:59

New England Patriots at 5:01

KICKOFF			9-L.Tynes kicks 69 yards from NYG 30 to NE 1. 39-L.Maroney pushed out of bounds at NE 44 for 43 yards (35-K.Dockery).
1-10	NE 44	4:52	12-T.Brady pass incomplete short right to 39-L.Maroney [96-B.Cofield].
2-10	NE 44	4:47	39-L.Maroney left tackle to NYG 47 for 9 yards (28-G.Wilson, 31-A.Ross).
3-1	NYG 47	4:03	NE 50-Vrabel eligible. 39-L.Maroney left tackle to NYG 42 for 5 yards (37-Ja.Butler).
1-10	NYG 42	3:30	12-T.Brady pass incomplete short middle to 10-J.Gaffney.
2-10	NYG 42	3:24	(Shotgun) 12-T.Brady pass short middle to 18-D.Stallworth to NYG 35 for 7 yards (55-K.Mitchell, 58-A.Pierce).
3-3	NYG 35	2:37	(Shotgun) 12-T.Brady pass short left to 83-W.Welker to NYG 27 for 8 yards (35-K.Dockery, 28-G.Wilson).
1-10	NYG 27	2:04	44-H.Evans up the middle to NYG 25 for 2 yards (98-F.Robbins).
2-8	NYG 25	1:24	(Shotgun) 12-T.Brady pass short right to 33-K.Faulk to NYG 17 for 8 yards (29-S.Madison).
1-10	NYG 17	:37	(Shotgun) 12-T.Brady pass incomplete short right to 84-B.Watson.
2-10	NYG 17	:32	(Shotgun) 12-T.Brady pass incomplete short right to 33-K.Faulk.
3-10	NYG 17	:29	(Shotgun) 12-T.Brady pass incomplete deep middle to 84-B.Watson [92-M.Strahan]. PENALTY on NYG-58-A.Pierce, Defensive Pass Interference, 16 yards, enforced at NYG 17 – No Play.
1-1	NYG 1	:23	NE 50-Vrabel eligible. 39-L.Maroney left tackle to NYG 1 for no gain (91-J.Tuck).

END OF FIRST QUARTER • NYG 3   NE 0

Super Bowl record: only 2 drives in 1st quarter

2nd Quarter

New England Patriots drive continues ...

2-1	NYG 1	15:00	NE 50-Vrabel eligible. 39-L.Maroney right guard for 1 yard, **TOUCHDOWN**.
EXTRA POINT			3-S.Gostkowski extra point is **GOOD**, Center-66-L.Paxton, Holder-6-C.Hanson.

NYG 3   NE 7   Plays: 12   Possession: 5:04

New York Giants at 14:57

KICKOFF			3-S.Gostkowski kicks 65 yards from NE 30 to NYG 5, out of bounds.
1-10	NYG 40	14:57	27-B.Jacobs up the middle to NYG 43 for 3 yards (75-V.Wilfork).
2-7	NYG 43	14:19	10-E.Manning pass incomplete short middle to 17-P.Burress (27-E.Hobbs).
3-7	NYG 43	14:11	(Shotgun) 10-E.Manning pass deep left to 81-A.Toomer ran out of bounds at NE 19 for 38 yards.

Brandon Jacobs carried the ball six times in the Giants' opening drive.

Gibril Wilson pressures Tom Brady on this attempted deep pass to Randy Moss.

SUPER BOWL XLII PLAY-BY-PLAY *continued*

Down/Yds.To Go	Ball On	Time	Decription of Play – (Tackle by), [Pressure by]
1-10	NE 19	14:03	27-B.Jacobs left guard to NE 15 for 4 yards (93-R.Seymour, 54-T.Bruschi).
2-6	NE 15	13:16	*PENALTY* on NYG-10-E.Manning, Delay of Game, 5 yards, enforced at NE 15 – No Play.
2-11	NE 20	12:50	(Shotgun) 10-E.Manning pass short right to 85-D.Tyree to NE 14 for 6 yards (22-A.Samuel).
3-5	NE 14	12:04	(Shotgun) 10-E.Manning pass short left intended for 12-S.Smith *INTERCEPTED* by 27-E.Hobbs at NE 10. 27-E.Hobbs pushed out of bounds at NE 33 for 23 yards (44-A.Bradshaw).

New England Patriots at 11:53

Down/Yds.To Go	Ball On	Time	Decription of Play – (Tackle by), [Pressure by]
1-10	NE 33	11:53	12-T.Brady pass short left to 39-L.Maroney to NE 41 for 8 yards (93-J.Alford).
2-2	NE 41	11:11	39-L.Maroney left end pushed out of bounds at NE 42 for 1 yard (72-O.Umenyiora).
3-1	NE 42	10:43	39-L.Maroney left tackle to NE 40 for -2 yards (37-Ja.Butler, 92-M.Strahan).
4-3	NE 40	10:04	6-C.Hanson punts 40 yards to NYG 20, Center-66-L.Paxton. 25-R.McQuarters to NYG 36 for 16 yards (58-P.Woods).

New York Giants at 9:51

Down/Yds.To Go	Ball On	Time	Decription of Play – (Tackle by), [Pressure by]
1-10	NYG 36	9:51	10-E.Manning sacked at NYG 33 for -3 yards (97-J.Green).
2-13	NYG 33	9:22	(Shotgun) 10-E.Manning *FUMBLES* (Aborted at NYG 32, *RECOVERED* by NYG-44-A.Bradshaw at NYG 30. 44-A.Bradshaw to NYG 30 for no gain (58-P.Woods).
3-16	NYG 30	8:49	(Shotgun) 10-E.Manning pass incomplete short right to 44-A.Bradshaw.
4-16	NYG 30	8:46	18-J.Feagles punts 55 yards to NE 15, Center-51-Z.DeOssie. 83-W.Welker to NE 30 for 15 yards (37-Ja.Butler).

New England Patriots at 8:35

Down/Yds.To Go	Ball On	Time	Decription of Play – (Tackle by), [Pressure by]
1-10	NE 30	8:35	39-L.Maroney up the middle to NE 30 for no gain (91-J.Tuck, 55-K.Mitchell).
2-10	NE 30	7:55	(Shotgun) 12-T.Brady sacked at NE 23 for -7 yards (55-K.Mitchell).
3-17	NE 23	7:19	(Shotgun) 12-T.Brady sacked at NE 16 for -7 yards (91-J.Tuck).
4-24	NE 16	6:54	6-C.Hanson punts 41 yards to NYG 43, Center-66-L.Paxton. 25-R.McQuarters pushed out of bounds at NYG 43 for no gain (52-E.Alexander).

New York Giants at 6:45

Down/Yds.To Go	Ball On	Time	Decription of Play – (Tackle by), [Pressure by]
1-10	NYG 43	6:45	27-B.Jacobs right guard to NYG 45 for 2 yards (54-T.Bruschi).
2-8	NYG 45	6:01	44-A.Bradshaw right tackle to NE 42 for 13 yards (37-R.Harrison).
1-10	NE 42	5:25	27-B.Jacobs right guard to NE 38 for 4 yards (54-T.Bruschi, 93-R.Seymour).
2-6	NE 38	4:40	27-B.Jacobs left guard to NE 31 for 7 yards (54-T.Bruschi).
1-10	NE 31	4:01	10-E.Manning pass short left to 44-A.Bradshaw to NE 28 for 3 yards (55-J.Seau), [95-R.Moore].
2-7	NE 28	3:14	44-A.Bradshaw right tackle to NE 25 for 3 yards (93-R.Seymour).
3-4	NE 25	2:31	(Shotgun) 10-E.Manning sacked at NE 32 for -7 yards (96-A.Thomas). *FUMBLES* (96-A.Thomas) [96-A.Thomas], touched at NE 29, *RECOVERED* by NYG-12-S.Smith at NE 20. 12-S.Smith pushed out of bounds at NE 20 for no gain (31-B.Meriweather). *PENALTY* on NYG-44-A.Bradshaw, Illegal Bat, 10 yards, enforced at NE 29.
3-18	NE 39	2:01	(Shotgun) 10-E.Manning pass incomplete deep left to 12-S.Smith (21-R.Gay).
			Two-Minute Warning
4-18	NE 39	1:54	18-J.Feagles punts 28 yards to NE 11, Center-51-Z.DeOssie, fair catch by 33-K.Faulk.

New England Patriots at 1:47

Down/Yds.To Go	Ball On	Time	Decription of Play – (Tackle by), [Pressure by]
1-10	NE 11	1:47	(Shotgun) 12-T.Brady pass incomplete deep left to 81-R.Moss [28-G.Wilson].
2-10	NE 11	1:41	39-L.Maroney right end to NE 8 for -3 yards (91-J.Tuck, 72-O.Umenyiora).
			Timeout #1 by NYG at 1:35.
3-13	NE 8	1:35	(Shotgun) 12-T.Brady pass short left to 18-D.Stallworth to NE 26 for 18 yards (58-A.Pierce).
1-10	NE 26	1:11	(Shotgun) 12-T.Brady pass incomplete deep right to 81-R.Moss [91-J.Tuck].
2-10	NE 26	1:05	(Shotgun) 33-K.Faulk up the middle to NE 41 for 15 yards (92-M.Strahan). *PENALTY* on NE-84-B.Watson, Offensive Holding, 10 yards, enforced at NE 33.
			Timeout #1 by NE at :59.
2-13	NE 23	:59	(Shotgun) 12-T.Brady pass short left to 83-W.Welker to NE 32 for 9 yards (98-F.Robbins, 91-J.Tuck).
3-4	NE 32	:35	(No Huddle, Shotgun) 12-T.Brady pass short left to 33-K.Faulk to NE 38 for 6 yards (35-K.Dockery).
			Timeout #2 by NE at :28.
1-10	NE 38	:28	(Shotgun) 12-T.Brady pass deep right to 81-R.Moss pushed out of bounds at NYG 44 for 18 yards (35-K.Dockery).
1-10	NYG 44	:22	(No Huddle, Shotgun) 12-T.Brady sacked at NE 49 for -7 yards (91-J.Tuck). *FUMBLES* (91-J.Tuck), *RECOVERED* by NYG-72-O.Umenyiora at NE 49. 72-O.Umenyiora to NE 49 for no gain (67-D.Koppen).

Down/ Yds.To Go	Ball On	Time	Decription of Play – (Tackle by), [Pressure by]

New York Giants at :10

| 1-10 | NE 49 | :10 | (Shotgun) 10-E.Manning pass incomplete short middle to 12-S.Smith. |

Timeout #3 by NE at :05.

| 2-10 | NE 49 | :05 | (Shotgun) 10-E.Manning pass incomplete deep right to 12-S.Smith. |

END OF SECOND QUARTER • NYG 3   NE 7

3rd Quarter

New England Patriots at 15:00

KICKOFF			9-L.Tynes kicks 65 yards from NYG 30 to NE 5. 39-L.Maroney to NE 21 for 16 yards (57-C.Blackburn, 43-M.Johnson).
1-10	NE 21	14:53	(Shotgun) 12-T.Brady pass short left to 83-W.Welker to NE 36 for 15 yards (37-Ja.Butler, 55-K.Mitchell), [92-M.Strahan].
1-10	NE 36	14:16	39-L.Maroney up the middle to NE 43 for 7 yards (37-Ja.Butler, 28-G.Wilson).
2-3	NE 43	13:41	12-T.Brady pass incomplete short right to 33-K.Faulk (92-M.Strahan).
3-3	NE 43	13:36	(Shotgun) 12-T.Brady pass short left to 33-K.Faulk to NE 48 for 5 yards (43-M.Johnson, 55-K.Mitchell), [72-O.Umenyiora].
1-10	NE 48	13:02	39-L.Maroney left end to NE 46 for -2 yards (72-O.Umenyiora).
2-12	NE 46	12:18	(Shotgun) 12-T.Brady pass short middle to 83-W.Welker to NYG 47 for 7 yards (58-A.Pierce, 55-K.Mitchell).
3-5	NYG 47	11:38	(Shotgun) 12-T.Brady pass short left to 33-K.Faulk to NYG 44 for 3 yards (58-A.Pierce).
4-2	NYG 44	11:07	(Punt formation) 6-C.Hanson punts 31 yards to NYG 13, Center-66-L.Paxton. 25-R.McQuarters ran out of bounds at NYG 14 for 1 yard. NE *CHALLENGED* the play, claiming too many players on field. Upon review, play was *REVERSED* resulting in a *PENALTY* on NYG-57-C.Blackburn, Defensive 12 On-field, 5 yards, enforced at NYG 44 – *No Play.*
1-10	NYG 39	11:00	12-T.Brady pass short left to 39-L.Maroney to NYG 35 for 4 yards (98-F.Robbins, 58-A.Pierce).

Super Bowl record: Tom Brady, most pass completions, career (84)

2-6	NYG 35	10:25	*PENALTY* on NE-72-M.Light, False Start, 5 yards, enforced at NYG 35 – No Play.
2-11	NYG 40	10:08	(Shotgun) 12-T.Brady pass short right to 83-W.Welker to NYG 42 for -2 yards (31-A.Ross, 23-C.Webster).
3-13	NYG 42	9:26	(Shotgun) 12-T.Brady pass short right to 33-K.Faulk to NYG 28 for 14 yards (28-G.Wilson , 58-A.Pierce).
1-10	NYG 28	8:42	39-L.Maroney right guard to NYG 28 for no gain (53-R.Torbor).
2-10	NYG 28	8:10	12-T.Brady pass short left to 88-K.Brady to NYG 25 for 3 yards (53-R.Torbor).
3-7	NYG 25	7:23	(Shotgun) 12-T.Brady sacked at NYG 31 for -6 yards (92-M.Strahan).
4-13	NYG 31	6:49	(Shotgun) 12-T.Brady pass incomplete deep left to 10-J.Gaffney.

New York Giants at 6:43

1-10	NYG 31	6:43	27-B.Jacobs left guard to NYG 35 for 4 yards (54-T.Bruschi, 93-R.Seymour).
2-6	NYG 35	6:06	10-E.Manning pass short right to 81-A.Toomer to NYG 45 for 10 yards (37-R.Harrison; 22-A.Samuel).
1-10	NYG 45	5:27	44-A.Bradshaw right guard to NYG 47 for 2 yards (75-V.Wilfork, 54-T.Bruschi).
2-8	NYG 47	4:42	(Shotgun) 10-E.Manning pass short right to 81-A.Toomer to NE 45 for 8 yards (36-J.Sanders).
1-10	NE 45	4:09	10-E.Manning pass incomplete deep middle to 17-P.Burress (22-A.Samuel).
2-10	NE 45	4:00	44-A.Bradshaw up the middle to NE 41 for 4 yards (37-R.Harrison).
3-6	NE 41	3:18	(Shotgun) 10-E.Manning pass incomplete short left to 17-P.Burress (21-R.Gay).
4-6	NE 41	3:12	18-J.Feagles punts 31 yards to NE 10, Center-51-Z.DeOssie, out of bounds.

New England Patriots at 3:04

1-10	NE 10	3:04	*PENALTY* on NE-84-B.Watson, False Start, 5 yards, enforced at NE 10 – No Play.
1-15	NE 5	3:04	(Shotgun) 12-T.Brady pass incomplete short left to 18-D.Stallworth.
2-15	NE 5	3:01	12-T.Brady pass short middle to 83-W.Welker to NE 21 for 16 yards (28-G.Wilson).
1-10	NE 21	2:19	39-L.Maroney right tackle to NE 30 for 9 yards (96-B.Cofield, 55-K.Mitchell).
2-1	NE 30	1:47	39-L.Maroney left end to NE 32 for 2 yards (72-O.Umenyiora).
1-10	NE 32	1:03	(Shotgun) 12-T.Brady pass short middle to 83-W.Welker to NYG 49 for 19 yards (37-Ja.Butler).
1-10	NYG 49	:17	(Shotgun) 12-T.Brady pass incomplete short right to 83-W.Welker.
2-10	NYG 49	:14	*PENALTY* on NE-72-M.Light, False Start, 5 yards, enforced at NYG 49 – No Play.
2-15	NE 46	:14	12-T.Brady pass incomplete deep right to 81-R.Moss.
3-15	NE 46	:06	(Shotgun) 12-T.Brady pass short left to 18-D.Stallworth to NYG 45 for 9 yards (37-Ja.Butler).

END OF THIRD QUARTER • NYG 3   NE 7

The Giants defense held the Patriots to just 45 rushing yards in Super Bowl XLII.

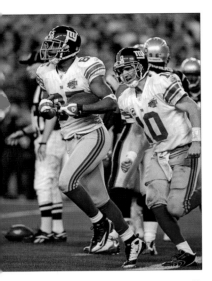

Eli and **David Tyree** come off after combining on a five-yard touchdown pass to give the Giants the lead early in the fourth quarter.

SUPER BOWL XLII PLAY-BY-PLAY *continued*

4th Quarter

Down/ Yds.To Go	Ball On	Time	Decription of Play – (Tackle by), [Pressure by]

New England Patriots drive continues ...

4-6	NYG 45	15:00	6-C.Hanson punts 45 yards to end zone, Center-66-L.Paxton, Touchback.

New York Giants at 14:52

1-10	NYG 20	14:52	10-E.Manning pass deep middle to 89-K.Boss to NE 35 for 45 yards (37-R.Harrison).
1-10	NE 35	14:02	44-A.Bradshaw right guard to NE 31 for 4 yards (54-T.Bruschi).
2-6	NE 31	13:16	44-A.Bradshaw left guard to NE 29 for 2 yards (93-R.Seymour, 54-T.Bruschi).
3-4	NE 29	12:34	(Shotgun) 10-E.Manning pass short middle to 12-S.Smith to NE 12 for 17 yards (31-B.Meriweather).
1-10	NE 12	11:54	(Shotgun) 44-A.Bradshaw up the middle to NE 5 for 7 yards (37-R.Harrison, 36-J.Sanders).
2-3	NE 5	11:10	10-E.Manning pass short middle to 85-D.Tyree for 5 yards, *TOUCHDOWN*.
EXTRA POINT			9-L.Tynes extra point is *GOOD*, Center-93-J.Alford, Holder-18-J.Feagles.

NYG 10   NE 7   Plays: 6   Possession: 3:47

New England Patriots at 11:05

KICKOFF			9-L.Tynes kicks 67 yards from NYG 30 to NE 3. 39-L.Maroney to NE 32 for 29 yards(58-A.Pierce, 59-G.Wilkinson). *PENALTY* on NE-71-R.Hochstein, OffensiveHolding, 10 yards, enforced at NE 21.
1-10	NE 11	10:59	12-T.Brady pass short right to 81-R.Moss to NE 28 for 17 yards (58-A.Pierce).
1-10	NE 28	10:26	(Shotgun) 12-T.Brady pass short left to 83-W.Welker to NE 31 for 3 yards (29-S.Madison).
2-7	NE 31	9:41	(Shotgun) 12-T.Brady pass incomplete deep left to 81-R.Moss.
3-7	NE 31	9:36	(Shotgun) 12-T.Brady pass incomplete short left to 83-W.Welker (29-S.Madison).
4-7	NE 31	9:30	6-C.Hanson punts 49 yards to NYG 20, Center-66-L.Paxton. 25-R.McQuarters pushed out of bounds at NYG 29 for 9 yards (53-L.Izzo).

New York Giants at 9:20

1-10	NYG 29	9:20	27-B.Jacobs up the middle to NYG 30 for 1 yard (94-T.Warren, 93-R.Seymour).
2-9	NYG 30	8:32	10-E.Manning pass incomplete deep left to 17-P.Burress.
3-9	NYG 30	8:24	(Shotgun) 10-E.Manning pass short middle to 81-A.Toomer to NYG 38 for 8 yards (37-R.Harrison).
4-1	NYG 38	8:02	18-J.Feagles punts 42 yards to NE 20, Center-51-Z.DeOssie, fair catch by 83-W.Welker.

New England Patriots at 7:54

1-10	NE 20	7:54	(Shotgun) 12-T.Brady pass short right to 83-W.Welker to NE 25 for 5 yards (55-K.Mitchell).
2-5	NE 25	7:19	(Shotgun) 12-T.Brady pass short right to 81-R.Moss to NE 35 for 10 yards (23-C.Webster).
1-10	NE 35	6:39	39-L.Maroney left end pushed out of bounds at NE 44 for 9 yards (37-Ja.Butler).
2-1	NE 44	6:14	12-T.Brady pass short right to 83-W.Welker to NYG 43 for 13 yards (58-A.Pierce, 37-Ja.Butler).
1-10	NYG 43	5:27	(Shotgun) 12-T.Brady pass short left to 33-K.Faulk pushed out of bounds at NYG 39 for 4 yards (58-A.Pierce).
2-6	NYG 39	5:01	(Shotgun) 12-T.Brady pass short left to 83-W.Welker to NYG 29 for 10 yards (37-Ja.Butler).

Super Bowl record: Wes Welker's 11th reception ties single-game record
shared with Dan Ross, Jerry Rice & Deion Branch

1-10	NYG 29	4:15	(Shotgun) 12-T.Brady pass incomplete short right to 18-D.Stallworth.
2-10	NYG 29	4:12	12-T.Brady pass short right to 81-R.Moss to NYG 18 for 11 yards (58-A.Pierce).
1-10	NYG 18	3:31	(Shotgun) 12-T.Brady pass short middle to 33-K.Faulk to NYG 6 for 12 yards (37-Ja.Butler). *NYG-98-F.Robbins was injured during the play.*
1-6	NYG 6	2:55	12-T.Brady pass incomplete short left to 81-R.Moss.
2-6	NYG 6	2:49	(Shotgun) 12-T.Brady pass incomplete short right to 83-W.Welker. *NYG-37-Ja.Butler was injured during the play.*
3-6	NYG 6	2:45	(Shotgun) 12-T.Brady pass short right to 81-R.Moss for 6 yards, *TOUCHDOWN*.
EXTRA POINT			3-S.Gostkowski extra point is *GOOD*, Center-66-L.Paxton, Holder-6-C.Hanson.

NYG 10   NE 14   Plays: 12   Possession: 5:12

Down/ Yds.To Go	Ball On	Time	Decription of Play – (Tackle by), [Pressure by]
New York Giants at 2:42			
KICKOFF			3-S.Gostkowski kicks 67 yards from NE 30 to NYG 3. 87-D.Hixon to NYG 17 for 14 yards (41-R.Ventrone).
1-10	NYG 17	2:39	(Shotgun) 10-E.Manning pass short right to 81-A.Toomer to NYG 28 for 11 yards (37-R.Harrison).
1-10	NYG 28	2:09	(No Huddle, Shotgun) 10-E.Manning pass incomplete short middle to 17-P.Burress.
2-10	NYG 28	2:04	(Shotgun) 10-E.Manning pass incomplete short left to 17-P.Burress.
			Two-Minute Warning
3-10	NYG 28	1:59	(Shotgun) 10-E.Manning pass short left to 81-A.Toomer to NYG 37 for 9 yards (37-R.Harrison).
4-1	NYG 37	1:34	27-B.Jacobs up the middle to NYG 39 for 2 yards (75-V.Wilfork, 93-R.Seymour).
1-10	NYG 39	1:28	(Shotgun) 10-E.Manning scrambles right tackle to NYG 44 for 5 yards (96-A.Thomas).
			Timeout #1 by NYG at 1:20.
2-5	NYG 44	1:20	(Shotgun) 10-E.Manning pass incomplete deep right to 85-D.Tyree.
3-5	NYG 44	1:15	(Shotgun) 10-E.Manning pass deep middle to 85-D.Tyree to NE 24 for 32 yards (37-R.Harrison).
			Timeout #2 by NYG at :59.
1-10	NE 24	:59	(Shotgun) 10-E.Manning sacked at NE 25 for -1 yards (96-A.Thomas).
			Timeout #3 by NYG at :51.
2-11	NE 25	:51	(Shotgun) 10-E.Manning pass incomplete short left to 85-D.Tyree (31-B.Meriweather).
3-11	NE 25	:45	(Shotgun) 10-E.Manning pass short right to 12-S.Smith pushed out of bounds at NE 13 for 12 yards (31-B.Meriweather).
1-10	NE 13	:39	(Shotgun) 10-E.Manning pass short left to 17-P.Burress for 13 yards, *TOUCHDOWN*.
EXTRA POINT			9-L.Tynes extra point is *GOOD*, Center-93-J.Alford, Holder-18-J.Feagles.

NYG 17   NE 14   Plays: 12   Possession: 2:07

Plaxico Burress holds the latest addition to his trophy case after scoring what would prove to be the Super-Bowl-winning touchdown.

Down/ Yds.To Go	Ball On	Time	Decription of Play – (Tackle by), [Pressure by]
New England Patriots at :35			
KICKOFF			9-L.Tynes kicks 61 yards from NYG 30 to NE 9. 39-L.Maroney to NE 26 for 17 yards (51-Z.DeOssie, 57-C.Blackburn).
1-10	NE 26	:29	(Shotgun) 12-T.Brady pass incomplete deep right to 10-J.Gaffney.
2-10	NE 26	:25	(Shotgun) 12-T.Brady sacked at NE 16 for -10 yards (93-J.Alford).
			Timeout #1 by NE at :19.
3-20	NE 16	:19	(Shotgun) 12-T.Brady pass incomplete deep left to 81-R.Moss (23-C.Webster).
			Timeout #2 by NE at :10.
4-20	NE 16	:10	(Shotgun) 12-T.Brady pass incomplete deep left to 81-R.Moss (28-G.Wilson).
New York Giants at :01			
1-10	NE 16	:01	10-E.Manning kneels at NE 17 for -1 yard.

END OF GAME   •   FINAL SCORE: NYG 17   NE 14

Photo Credits

AP Photo/Bill Kostroun – 153.

John Paul Filo/CBS/*The Late Show With David Letterman* – 110 (right).

Getty Images – Al Bello: 144, 146, 148; 149 (top), 150. Doug Benc: 21, 111. Scott Boehm: endpapers, 2-3, 65 (top), 101. Scott Cunningham: 26, 27. Jonathan Daniel: 65 (bottom). Diamond Images: 36. David Drapkin: 22. Greg Flume: 37, 38. Stu Forster: 104. Larry French: 10-11, 87, 89. Chris Graythen: 92, 95, 97. Scott Halleran: 113 (bottom). Drew Hallowell: 7, 15. Tom Hauck: 72, 130. Wesley Hitt: 90-91. Harry How: 57-59, 98-99, 115. Paul Jasienski: 74-76, 78. Streeter Lecka: 137. G. Newman Lowrance: 44, 62 (right). Donald Miralle: 13, 132, 141. Doug Pensinger: 134, 135. Evan Pinkus: 32, 34, 88 (top), 94, 151. Joe Robbins: 93. Paul Spinelli: 66, 96, 122, 124, 131. Rick Stewart: 77. David Stluka: 64. Rob Tringali, 152. Dilip Vishwanat: 68. Thomas E. Witte: 49 (bottom). Jeff Zelevansky: 69

INFPhoto/JaeDonnelly – 112 (left).

NFL Photos/Getty Images – Ben Liebenberg: 136.

Christopher Pope Photography – 8, 9, 12, 14, 17-20, 28-31, 33, 35, 39-43, 45-48, 49 (top), 50-56, 60, 61, 62 (left), 63, 65 (top), 70, 71, 73, 79-86, 88 (bottom), 100, 101 (bottom), 102-103, 105-109, 110 (left), 112 (right), 113 (top), 114, 116-121, 123, 126-128, 133, 136 (inset), 138, 140, 142-143, 149 (bottom, left and right), 155-160.

Schinder family photo – 145.

Sports Illustrated/Getty Images – Robert Beck: 139. John Biever: 67. Greg Nelson: 23-25. Bob Rosato: 1, 129.